3

Swallow the Ocean

Sally and Laura in 1972

Swallow
the Ocean

A M E M O I R

Laura M. Flynn

C O U N T E R P O I N T • B E R K E L E Y

Copyright © 2008 by Laura M. Flynn

AUTHOR'S NOTE: This story is drawn from memories of real events that took place over thirty years ago. Most names, except for those of my immediate family, have been changed. In telling this story I have tried to be truthful, and where possible to verify my recollections against those of others. Nevertheless, memory is not only imperfect, it is a gifted editor, constantly compressing and expanding images of the past into something far more shapely than life as it was lived.

Library of Congress Cataloging-in-Publication Data

Flynn, Laura M., 1966–
  Swallow the ocean : a memoir / Laura M. Flynn.
    p. cm.
  ISBN-13: 978-1-58243-385-1
  ISBN-10: 1-58243-385-2
1. Flynn, Laura M., 1966– 2. Children of parents with mental disabilities
—California—San Francisco—Biography. 3. Mentally ill parents—
California—San Francisco—Biography. I. Title.

RC464.F69A3 2007
616.890092—dc22
[B]   2007033247

Cover design by Nicole Caputo
Interior design by Gopa & Ted2, Inc.
Printed in the United States of America

COUNTERPOINT • 2117 Fourth Street • Suite D • Berkeley, CA 94710

Distributed by Publishers Group West   10 9 8 7 6 5 4 3 2 1

For my sisters, Sara and Amy
For my father, Russell Flynn
And for my mother, Sally Ann Flynn

For why do our thoughts turn to some gesture of a hand, the fall of a sleeve, some corner of a room on a particular anonymous afternoon, even when we are asleep, even when we are so old that our thoughts have abandoned other business? What are all these fragments for, if not to be knit up finally?

—Marilynne Robinson, *Housekeeping*

Swallow the Ocean

San Francisco—1976

When I was nine my mother explained the world to me.

"There's a battle," she said, "between good and evil. And some of us—the strong—have a special role to play."

I was home alone with her—my father had moved out a year earlier and my two sisters were both at school. I was not really sick—no fever, no throwing up, no stuffed-up nose, just a vague bodily unease that convinced my mother to keep me home from school. We sat together on a clear spot on the floor in the front hall, looking at the faces on the dollar bills and coins in front of us. The mess that had been steadily overtaking every surface in the apartment since my father left stretched before us in all directions. Mail had accumulated near the front door, first on the shelves of the console table, but now it extended in unstable piles along the wall halfway to the living room, which was in turn a confusion of color and texture. Layers of clothing, papers, and toys blanketed the floor. Books pulled off the

shelves but not put back circled the bookshelves. Records—
some exposed, some in their white slips, some still in the album
covers—fanned out in a widening arc at the foot of the stereo.
Near the couches, fat metal knitting needles, holding twenty
or so uneven lines of scarf, were jammed into balls of yarn—
projects my older sister Sara and I had abandoned.

"Everyone who has ever lived is still with us," my mother
said, pushing her glasses higher up on her nose. A piece of
Scotch tape held them together at the corner. The faces of these
men on the coins and bills in front of us, circulating among us,
had an impact on people and events, for better and for worse,
she explained. She was in touch with some of them, the good
ones.

"Like Abraham Lincoln?" I ventured.

"No," she said. "He's good, but not strong enough."

I was a little put out on Lincoln's behalf. He seemed like the
best of the lot to me. He'd freed the slaves and his little boy had
died, which made me feel protective.

"Who's good and strong?" I asked.

She paused a moment, then said, "George Washington." She
handed me a dollar bill.

He looked a little mean to me, Washington, and his white
curls, odd. But I could see what she was getting at—he had that
firm set to his lips.

She picked a silver dollar up off the floor and handed it to
me. "John Kennedy is the most powerful."

Certainly, Kennedy was a powerful presence in our lives.
You couldn't wade through the living room without tripping

over a book with his face on the cover. Whenever we were close to Golden Gate Park, my mother would drive up and down the boulevard that was named for him. Sometimes she made a special trip just to drive the full length of it, from the panhandle all the way out to Ocean Beach. She found a special gold-plated JFK commemorative half-dollar in the gift shop of the mint when she dragged me there for a tour. The coin was carved out so only Kennedy's square-jawed profile hung inside a gold ring. She wore it now on a slim gold chain, replacing the heavy gold cross that had lain at the point of her clavicle for as long as I could remember.

"He's my special partner," she said.

I didn't like the sound of "special partner." Not at all. There was something wrong about it.

"He helps me," she continued. I didn't want to hear any more. And yet.

"Helps you what?" I asked.

"He helps me fight the devils," she said.

I blinked, but kept going. "How?"

She rubbed a half-dollar between her fingers, searching for words, to describe what she knew I couldn't see.

"I stretch them out in my mind," she said. She held her fingers together, then drew them slowly apart, the way you might stretch taffy or bubble gum. "I stretch them until they're destroyed."

I watched her fingers slowly come apart and could see how the devils would be—solid at first like pieces of unchewed bubble gum, becoming elastic as they stretched, then turning to long filaments that finally broke and disintegrated as you pulled them apart.

I had a special place in my head for the things my mother told me. I knew a thing could be real and not real at the same time. I was a big reader—I took in what she told me like a book or a story, undiluted, caught up in the moment of the telling. I wanted details. I wanted to understand how it all worked. Whether what she told me was real or not almost didn't matter. This was all treacherously real to her, and she took any sign of skepticism as betrayal. I lived in her world, and even if none of this was real to other people, the consequences were real for me.

She talked on and on. The weather, earthquakes, Vietnam, Patty Hearst, Squeaky Fromme, the signs of the times. Everything counted; everything was in play. A monumental shift was under way, right now as she spoke, and she was at the heart of it.

"There is no one else," she said. "I have a role no one can fill." Her pale blue eyes fixed on me from behind the thick glasses, waiting for a reply.

I nodded my assent. Her eyes slipped away. I felt relief. She gazed down the hall, past me, towards the front windows in the living room, her own head nodding up and down intently.

Sitting there on the floor next to her, asking questions, my body, eyes, and voice must have reflected the same simple faith in her that I'd always felt, but a part of me was already backing away, edging towards the front door, slowly, the way you move away from a dangerous animal so it won't startle.

PART ONE *Riptide*

Chapter One—1972

"PICK A NUMBER between one and ten," my mother said, squeezing her wide-set blue eyes shut. She wasn't wearing glasses. She rarely did back then—vanity, I suppose. I stopped on the path, closed my eyes, and waited for the number to whisper itself in my ear.

"One," said Amy.

"Seven," I blurted out.

"That's right!" my mother said, her eyes opening in surprise. "You're getting good at this."

We played this game to sort things out—who went first, who sat up front, who got the extra cookie—but also to hone our psychic abilities. Practice, my mother said, practice was the key.

When I was five and my sister Amy was still a toddler, we lived just half a block from Golden Gate Park. On sunny afternoons when I got home from kindergarten, while my father was at work and my sister Sara still at school, my mother rolled out the Wonder Chair—our big lug of a stroller with dangerous joints and a heavy vinyl seat—and shepherded us across Fulton Street, into the Rose Garden, and through the park for the elaborate series of visits and stops that had become our ritual.

Somehow in my memory it is always late spring, after the cherry blossoms but before the summer tourists. I don't remember the rainy days, and these sunny afternoons have united to form a single walk through the park.

In the Rose Garden my mother released Amy from the stroller, and the three of us bounced from flower to flower, closing in on the strongest-scented roses. Couples sprawled on the grass between the rows of plants, girls in gauzy skirts entwined in the arms of long-haired boys. On the benches, old women in straight tweedy skirts pressed their heels and lips together in disapproval. My mother fell somewhere in between this cultural divide.

She saw herself as something of a bohemian. My parents, both Midwesterners, had come to San Francisco together to lay down fresh tracks, to leave behind the narrowness and provincialism of their childhoods. My mother in particular believed that here, in this most European of American cities, she could make all the choices about our lives, from where we went to school to what we ate, read, and believed.

At just past thirty, my mother was tall and slim, taller seeming than her five feet seven, perhaps because she usually wore heels, even for a walk in the park. Her eyes—large, brilliant blue, inherited from her mother and passed on to me and my sisters—were her defining feature, all the more striking for being set against her pale skin and dark hair. She had a slight overbite, visible when she smiled, and low pronounced cheekbones. She was beautiful, but from the evidence of the photos that survive, I'd have to say her beauty was somewhat unreliable: one day she was striking, the next, just strikingly pale.

The ladies on the benches always smiled when they saw us coming, my mother in her skirt and low-heeled pumps, leading two neatly dressed little girls, the Wonder Chair anchoring us firmly to the middle class. Amy might have been wearing one of the bright red or blue wool coats, with a matching bonnet that my mother favored when we were very small. I was bigger and the 1970s had dawned, so for me, at least, this look had given way to wide-legged plaid pants, cotton turtlenecks, and cardigans misbuttoned at the chest.

My mother never acknowledged the smiles of the ladies on the bench. Nor did she approve of the young people in the grass. For all her desire to throw off convention, she retained some of her Midwestern preacher's daughter sensibilities. She was always a little scandalized by the flesh and free love so brazenly on display in the San Francisco of my childhood.

We drifted through the roses in our own world, staying upwind of the young people on the grass and out of earshot of the ladies on the bench. My mother had an uncanny ability to create a private universe. We lived at the heart of a cultural maelstrom—I was born in 1966, the summer before the summer of love, just a block from Golden Gate Park. By 1972 the flower children had camped and decamped, the Vietnam War was still raging. And yet the San Francisco of my memory is almost unpeopled.

Our business in the Rose Garden was not to scandalize or be scandalized. We came for the flowers.

"This one is a *Roman Holiday*," my mother said. I made her read all the names on the little black plaques. *Tranquility, Artistry, Sea of Peace, Elegantyne, Golden Fleece, French Lace, Lavender Lassie, Soleil d'Or*. We practiced the French pronunciation. She brought her teeth together and rolled out the throaty *R* for me to copy. The skin on her neck trembled.

She spoke French, and that, along with the tales she told of sailing to Europe on the *Queen Mary* when she was young, of living in Paris, and of meeting my father on the steps of her hotel, suffused her with romance.

I liked to imagine her on the deck of the ship the day she sailed, unfurling streamers to the crowd below, dressed for the occasion, looking like a movie star, the way she looked in her college graduation picture, hair cut short, blue eyes glittering, in a tight-waisted, full-skirted dress, with a short string of pearls at her throat.

"I cried and cried that day," she would always say when she told me this story. The way she said it, I knew it was not just a little sniffling. She said she cried from the time she prepared to board the ship until the aunt and uncle who saw her off that day made their way down the gangplank.

This didn't fit. Her crying ruined the picture. This was an adventure story, a romance. She set off to see the world. She met and fell in love with my father in Paris and then had us.

Her story had a happy ending—the crying at the start was all wrong.

"Why did you cry?" I asked her.

She paused, as if trying to locate this lost moment in time. "I wasn't ever going to come back," she said, offering up this second, enigmatic, bit of information without explanation. I don't think I ever questioned her about it, but it troubled me. Here was the downside of her larger-than-lifeness, the hard-headed, no return, we-don't-do-things-like-other-people part of her. To me, her not wanting to come home seemed disloyal to my kindly grandparents, to my father, but most of all to my sisters and myself, whose existence depended on her willingness to come back and take up her life as wife and mother. In the self-preserving sophism of childhood, that was the only fate she was allowed.

The path turned sharply downhill just before we reached the Tea Garden. My mother relaxed her hold on the stroller, and we were all pulled into a run. We went headlong down the hill, tumbling forward at a speed on the outer edge of my mother's control. I hung on to the metal bar of the stroller. We arrived breathless and laughing at the wooden gate of the Tea Garden. There the path flattened out. The Wonder Chair rolled to a stop. We left it by the gate and entered the garden.

Amy and I raced along the stone paths in a carefully mani-cured world of dwarf trees, fishponds, wooden bridges, and torii gates. We stretched our legs to land squarely on the large stones. My right hand traveled the smooth surface of the low bamboo rail as I ran. We made our way quickly to the base of the moon bridge near the front entrance of the garden. I slowed down when I reached the spot where the path crossed the channeled water. Amy was so close she bumped up against me before coming to a stop.

I looked back and, not seeing my mother, I squatted by the pond and bent my head low. I nestled my chin in the cup formed by my up-tilted knees and surveyed the multilayered murkiness of the pond. Silver and copper coins shone up from the bottom. The rims and edges, half exposed under a light cover of silt, caught the sun. Above the coins a bright orange carp traversed the shallow waterway. At a distance, at a glance, the carp were beautiful, but kneeling here, up close, I thought they seemed too big, overgrown, their faces grotesque.

I studied the shadowy limbs of the water striders. They walked on water, "like Jesus," my mother said. Mostly they floated, moved only by the slight current of a breeze. Out of nowhere one of them would shoot across the pond, setting the others off in a skittery flash of movement. Then they were still again on the smooth surface of the water. The thing about water striders is, if you mess with them, if they get wet, even a single drop, they go under. They are held up by the surface tension. They don't know how to swim.

My mother took up her spot on the path directly across from the high wooden bridge and trained her whole attention on us. Once she was in place, Amy and I raced to the top, climbing the steep side of the wooden arch as if it were a ladder. We scrambled past grownups, the season's first tourists, slow-moving obstacles, people not fortunate enough to live in San Francisco, people who did not have sweaters tied around their waists and who would soon be chilled by the afternoon wind, people who struggled in their shorts up the vertical slope of the bridge. We were agile because the incline was better suited to a child's body and because this was our place. We were native San Franciscans, and this, my mother let us know, made us a little bit better than other people.

On top of the bridge I felt like a giant straddling the earth. The wood curved down and away under my feet in both directions. I clutched a penny in my hand and waited for my mother to look up. She stood on the path below. Her gaze fell loosely about her, fixed for a moment on something in the low hedge beside her, then moved out across the pond. Looking up, she smiled and called, "Make a wish." I squeezed my eyes shut and turned to toss the penny over my shoulder. I heard it plunk into the shallow pond. I turned around, looking first to my mother. She drew her hands up close to her face, clapping to signal her approval. Then my eyes searched for the penny. I saw only the sediment slowly rising, spreading, then just as slowly settling back down onto the bottom of the pond.

I edged my way down the side of the bridge, and my mother came to meet me. Holding out a hand, she braced me so I could jump from the second-to-last step. Amy came down backwards, her toddler body hugging the bridge, each foot in a blind search for the step below. My mother hovered behind her with both arms raised, resisting the urge to help, but prepared to break the fall.

We went down to the pond to see the ducks we had been following since early spring. My mother drew a plastic bag filled with bread crusts from inside her purse. The mother duck appeared with five babies trailing behind her. Her heather-gray feathers circled back in a pattern of light and dark, coming together in the final thrust of her tail. She stayed close to the shore, gliding through the reeds so that the ducklings moved in and out of sight. They picked the bread we tossed them off the surface of the water. I imagined myself coming back a mother duck in another life, coursing through the water, propelled by feet unseen.

Our last stop before tea was the bronze Buddha, set in his alcove at the top of a steep set of stairs. "He's holy, just like Jesus," my mother said.

I didn't think he was like Jesus at all. He was sturdy and smiling and he sat up very straight. Jesus, most times I had seen him, was skinny, stretched, hanging on the cross, skin pulled against his ribs, head drooping onto his chest, eyes full of suffering. Buddha was not like that. He was calmness cast in bronze. You didn't have to feel sorry for Buddha.

My mother read from the placard, "He is known as the Buddha who sits through sunny and rainy weather without shade." Amy and I each picked a flower from the azalea bush at his side. My mother lifted us, in turn, to reach up and place a single pink blossom on his upturned palm.

We had the teahouse nearly to ourselves. The wooden sandals of the Japanese women in kimonos who served the tea clattered on the concrete floor. They took tiny steps, toes gripping the wood of their sandals through white socks that puckered around the thong. I cracked open the two wings of my fortune cookie. It split like a wishbone into uneven halves. I slid the white strip of paper through the opening in the shell, careful not to tear it. Lips moving, I read my fortune slowly to myself. I could already read—I don't remember learning, just that at some point before I went to kindergarten the letters above my mother's fingertips had drawn themselves together and formed words for me.

The fortune can only have been good. Or if it wasn't, I passed the paper to my mother and waited while she held it close to her eyes to read. With her head cocked to the side, she'd think a moment and then reinterpret the fortune in my favor.

We ate the salty rice crackers, smooth as the lacquered table before us, and played past lives. My mother was quite taken with reincarnation; she let us try on former selves like Halloween costumes. Sometimes you were a squirrel; sometimes you were a boy. Amy, we all agreed, had recently been a tiger because she had a nasty bite. In another life, my mother said, I might be the mother and she the child. Each of us had a soul, precious and indestructible, the part of ourselves that would carry on and over into the next life. This she was sure of; this we could count on. I imagined mine as a small white cloud, something like Casper the friendly ghost, able, should need arise, to float out of my body and on down the street.

My mother reached over and ran a hand through my shoulder-length hair, tucking some stray ends behind my left ear. Amy wiggled in her seat. I held out my hand to my mother. "Read my palm," I said, hoping for something more substantial about my future. She took my hand and held it up in the sunlight. My palm and fingers were covered with a maze of lines, like an old woman's. "You've lived many lives," my mother said, not for the first time. She traced the deep line that circled my thumb. "This is your life line. You're going to have a long life." Then she moved her fingernail lightly across the straight line that crossed my palm. "This is your love line," she said. "It's a deep one."

Then we begged for stories from her childhood, or, best of all, "the story of when you and Daddy met." She always obliged.

It was 1960. She was living in Paris at a small Left Bank hotel. She and Mary, her friend from college who'd traveled with her on the *Queen Mary*, were coming down the stairs of the hotel, headed out to a jazz club or a bar and dressed for it—no doubt navigating the steep staircase as women in heels do, each foot wavering for a moment in the air before locating the next step. As they came to the landing on the second floor, a door stood open, blocking their passage. They stopped. My mother peered around the doorjamb into the room. Her eyes locked with my father's for the first time. He smiled and told her she could only pass if she agreed to have dinner. She smiled back and stepped gamely over the threshold.

My mother must have told us this story a thousand times. For her, for us, this was the moment, the hinge, the fateful coincidence upon which the rest of our lives turned. And we lapped it up: the open door, the romance of Paris nights, the not-so-subtle idea that some force in the universe was bending events in our favor.

Why not? We were lucky that way: born in this most beautiful of cities, our future on the whispering sliver of paper pulled from the fortune cookie, bread for the ducks, a penny for the pond, the storing of good deeds for the next life. With the weightless motion of the water striders, we moved on the bright plane of our existence. And, of course, we thought my mother walked on water.

The subdued sweetness of the fortune cookie melted into the saltiness of the rice crackers. A blackbird flew onto the counter, then under the table to clean our crumbs from the cement floor. I looked down and saw two pairs of small feet in matching white sandals, dangling in the air. My mother's legs were crossed, ladylike, at the knee, so that her right foot was suspended. Her shoe was coming off slightly at the heel. She stretched out her toe, angled it towards me and placed it just under the sole of my sandal. She tapped lightly, raising my foot and holding it for just a second in the air. Then, gently, she let it fall so that our feet bounced together in time.

Chapter Two

EACH HOUSE on our block had a narrow but deep yard in back. Many were paved for simple upkeep. Ours was not; we had dirt, some grass, and orange and pink geraniums for making and decorating mud pies on summer days when the fog went away. We had a small swing-set with poles painted red and white, which my father had just put together for my fifth birthday. But mostly the yard was mud and flowers.

A blade of grass in hand, I sought out and worried potato bugs into perfect black balls. I would block their path, lift them in the air, and place them back on ground they didn't recognize, until they curled into beady retreat. Then I rolled them across the tight packed dirt of the yard, onto the cement pathway, until, remembering the being inside the ball, I felt sorry. I would stop and sit perfectly still, waiting and watching, willing the potato bug to be brave again.

Squatting on the ground, huddled deep within myself, I

watched the floaters—airborne dust bunnies caught on the wind—mesmerized, as they drifted like sunspots across my vision. Sometimes I would look down at my own hand, and an odd feeling would run through me. *I am me,* I'd tell myself. This is my hand, my body, my life. *Laura,* I'd think, *I'm Laura.* This yard, this block, this family. How odd. Not that my life felt odder than anyone else's. It was the oddity of life itself. The everydayness of it, the get-up-and-walk-to-schoolness of it. Or, perhaps more precisely, it was the disconnect between this and that, between in here and out there. The self I knew best was holed up in my head, imagining, thinking, worrying over the potato bug. This was deeply familiar. To imagine this inner self as the owner of that hand was a stretch. Not a bad feeling. Not a good feeling. Just a sharp jolt of recognition.

I held my hand still on the ground in the path of bright red ladybugs until they tickled onto my finger. I raised them to my eyes and examined their uneven black spots. Then, unable to resist the urge, I cried, "Ladybug, ladybug, fly away home, your house is on fire and your children are all alone." The ladybug opened her red shell, splitting in a line straight down her back, and unfurled flimsy black wings. Chastened, she flew away.

What I did not do was to take a mirror or a magnifying glass and burn black beetles on the sidewalk. The Mulligans, who lived in the small blue house near the corner, who terrorized and utterly dominated our block, did this. My sisters and I watched in horror. Such straightforward cruelty. Boys really were rotten, made out of cotton and so on. But then, they played by an entirely different set of rules. The rightness or wrongness of their actions did not preoccupy their imaginations as it did ours. Which is not to say we were not cruel. We might exact a slow simmering toll, toy with a thing and test it, but never did we focus the sun's rays directly on a thing so it burned. But then, these boys were not my mother's children. If I felt remorse at torturing the potato bug, it was because I knew that her "do unto others" extended to even these.

My mother was, after all, a preacher's daughter. She was born in Wood River, Illinois, in 1937, the eldest of five, followed closely by four brothers, and, according to my grandfather, their "almost perfect child," "smart as a whip." She spent her childhood as the darling of her father's congregations, watching him in the pulpit every Sunday, first from her mother's lap and then from her own seat up front in the children's choir.

My mother's father, Amos, both demanded and commanded respect. Charming, charismatic, overbearing, he saw his own life as a morality tale, to be shared with children, grandchildren, family, or friends—anyone in need of moral instruction. He'd been a farm boy in rural Missouri, a ruffian, he claimed, who was saved by the grace of God. He was already eighteen the first time he entered a church—and he'd only come so he could play basketball for the church team. He stayed because that first Sunday he'd spotted my grandmother, Sadie, the minister's daughter, in the front row of the choir. Their courtship lasted several years and paralleled Amos's conversion. One night, already engaged to Sadie, alone in his room, he saw the light. I mean by this that he literally saw light. Afterwards, on his knees at the side of his bed, he asked God's forgiveness for his sins and promised to give his life over to the ministry if God would open the way for his education.

God apparently did. Amos and Sadie were married, and somehow in the darkest years of the Depression, taking heavy course loads and working road construction jobs in the summers to feed his growing family, Amos managed to plow through college and the seminary in six years. On the strength of his oratory he was called to his first pastorate in a large, prestigious Baptist church, while still a student at Eastern Baptist Seminary in Philadelphia.

Not a fire-and-brimstone Baptist, Amos tended towards a more intellectual, highbrow Christianity. But he had a strong authoritarian streak and a great affinity for the apostle Paul, which included subscribing to Paul's doctrine on women: as Christ is the head of the church, so man is the head of the family and so on—hardly a novel position in the Christian culture of the 1940s and 1950s in which my mother was raised.

By the early 1970s, we may have been living in free-love San Francisco, but not much had really changed. On our block, at least, all the mothers stayed home and the fathers worked. My father left each day, briefcase in hand, black oxfords on his feet, to walk to his real estate office just three blocks away. Sara and I, lunchboxes in hand, walked together to our elementary school five blocks away. On weekends we helped my father wash his car in the driveway. On Sunday we went to the imperial-looking Episcopal church on Nob Hill, dressed in white tights and Mary Janes.

My mother was mostly home with my sister Amy, who was just two. When my mother decided to go back to school, taking graduate classes at a nearby college and leaving Amy in the care of a cleaning lady who came three times a week, it seemed a radical thing to do.

We lived in the fog-prone Richmond district, built just after the 1906 earthquake, as San Francisco expanded out over the sand dunes towards the Pacific. These orderly blocks were the closest thing San Francisco had to suburbs. Our street was lined with two-story Edwardian row houses, with big front windows and no front yards. Just stoops that gave way to a very wide span of concrete crawling with children—for in those pre-stranger-danger days, the street was where we lived.

On the sidewalk in front of our house I tested my balance, the training wheels of my brand-new bicycle steadying me as I rode. Then I began to pedal long, smooth circles. One foot pressed, the other floated, alternating left and right, between effort and ease. The soles of my tennis shoes were thin enough that I could feel the flatness of the two bars beneath the curve of my arches. The pedals gained momentum, the clicking of the wheels turned to a whir, and I sailed away from our stoop.

Midway down the block, my sister Sara was playing hopscotch with her best friend, Celia Jeffers. Sara held her arms stiff and close to her body as she jumped through the boxes chalked out in pink and yellow on the sidewalk. She landed twice on one foot, then on two, then one, and then precariously she leapt over the square where her marker had fallen. Her dark hair flew behind her as she jumped. The red plastic knobs on the elastic that held the bangs she was growing out bounced and slid a little farther off-center as the hair worked itself loose. In one final double-hopping lunge, she staggered out of the box.

Sara was eight. I was five. Despite the age difference, I considered her my best friend. At home, she mostly played along, allowing me to co-star and co-conspire in the doll games we played in the sunroom in the back of our house. On the street my status was sadly reduced. I approached Sara and Celia tentatively, slowing down and circling once, awkwardly navigating the tight turn around the tree in front of Celia's house. I studied their faces for signs of welcome. Celia glanced over at me blankly, hard blue eyes under curly red hair. Sara collected her marker but did not look up at me. I pushed off quickly with one foot and began pedaling hard, trying to look as if I had only slowed but never intended to stop.

I wasn't allowed to cross the street, so I circled the four sides of our city block over and over again. Once on every trip I had to pass the Mulligans' house near the corner. Halfway down the block, the sticky dread began to rise. I tightened my grip, bent my head down low between the tall handlebars, and pedaled hard to build up speed. There were ten Mulligans, all boys except one. An endless horde of Patricks, Eddies, and Bobs in toughskin jeans and beefy tees; it was impossible to know one from the other. Sheer numbers gave them enough force to rule the neighborhood. They were tough to boot, and made us all feel utterly bullied and small. The black lines of bicycle skids and the ashy remains of redcaps and Chinese fire snakes strewn on the pavement marked the territory in front of their house.

Mulligans lurked unseen inside the garage or hidden behind a planter box on the circular stairway that led to their front door. They came from nowhere, bees from the hive, kamikazes on mean, low-to-the-ground boy bikes, pedals pounding furiously, not in circles at all, but in a brutal one-two that sent them crashing over curbs and popping wheelies across my path. A rubber band zinged before me, just missing my bare arm. The taunting Mulligan singsong rang out for the whole neighborhood to hear. "Training wheel baby, born in the navy." I steeled myself. My brain pumped words—sticks and stones may break my bones, sticks and stones may break my bones—coming up with the wrong half of my mother's mantra. Mostly I pumped the pedals hard; once I rounded the corner, the assault would end. The Mulligans were territorial, but they never gave chase.

Three blocks of solitude lay before me. As I turned the corner, the sidewalk narrowed, slowing me automatically as I navigated between driveways to my left and tightly pruned sycamore trees to the right. The trees ran the full length of the block, each planted neatly in a cube of dirt the size of one square of pavement. Going up Cabrillo Avenue, I pedaled due west. The ocean was directly in front of me, though I couldn't see it. The sun was setting through the fog. The whole sky was a hushed pink.

I took my time sailing up Cabrillo and gliding down Funston. Floating, falling, floating, falling, I pedaled long slow circles and settled into myself. The final short block was opposite Golden Gate Park. The towering fir trees in the park cast a dark gloom, but I felt safe on my side of the street, out here, where I knew no one and was not known.

Only when I turned the corner back onto our block did I feel a shift. I stopped pedaling, coasted a bit, suspended for a moment between the quiet exhilaration of solitude and the warmth and safety of home. Somewhere inside, my mother was making dinner and would soon call me in. She was always at the center of the orbit I was tracing, and if I had the courage to venture to the far side of the block, the grim determination to pedal through Mulligan territory alone, it was because I knew she was there.

My grandmother Sadie occupied the center of my mother's childhood as surely as my mother occupied mine. When I knew her, Sadie was a small, rounded woman, with a beautiful halo of perfectly white hair, bright clear blue eyes, and a sunny and sentimental temperament. Sadie had lived her entire life within the bounds of church and family. She never wavered from her faith, and she dedicated her entire life to her husband and children. And this is the kicker: she did it, for the most part, joyfully. My mother's only problem with Sadie was that, given her own temperament, her strong will, her aspirations, there was little in Sadie's life to give direction to her own. Growing up within the girdled prison of the feminine mystique, my mother probably had a hard time putting her finger on her discontent, but something rankled.

In high school my mother rebelled in all the predictable ways. Her grades plummeted; she took up with the son of the town drunk, "a disreputable fellow," according to my grandfather. She smoked and drank and climbed out her bedroom window at night to meet her boyfriend. She announced to her parents that she did not intend to go to college, implying that she would marry this "ne'er-do-well." It's hard to know just how bad she really was. Since she was the eldest, my grandparents had no experience with teenagers. They allowed no alcohol in the house, and my grandmother, also a minister's daughter, wasn't allowed to dance when she was growing up; it wouldn't have taken much to shake her.

Over the years Amos had made extra money for the family working on road construction crews during the summers, often making more in a single summer than he did from a year of preaching. In 1955, Amos left the ministry and, along with his older brother, started a road equipment and building company. Buoyed by the massive public investments made in the interstate highway system in the 1950s, Barton Construction, which Amos staffed with brothers, sons, and nephews, built roads from Florida to Michigan, elevating his family from a threadbare preacher's life to very well-to-do almost overnight. The family moved to a large remodeled house in Normal, Illinois. My grandfather had a "fleet plan" with Ford Motor Company. In 1959 he bought an airplane, which he used for business, but also for hunting trips; the boys learned to fly.

My mother did go to college in the end—to Knox College, a small liberal arts college founded by abolitionists in Galesburg, Illinois—and there she managed to keep up not only her grades but an active social and sorority girl life. By the time she graduated she was restless and alienated, and the future was rapidly closing in on her. She'd picked up on the undercurrents of distress with the culture of conformity that was America in the 1950s. No one was saying anything about "the system" yet—no one she knew, anyway. The movements that would name the sense of suffocation she felt were yet to be born.

She taught elementary school for a year in Chicago. Teaching was never her passion, more a safe harbor, a respectable way station for a well-educated girl until she got married. At the end of that year she decided she couldn't face another year of teaching. She had boyfriends and proposals but was adamant about not getting married. She didn't want to go home and work for her father. She was face-to-face with the limits of middle-class femininity in 1959 America. She seized upon the idea of a trip to Europe as her escape. I doubt she knew exactly what she was looking for—a measure of freedom, romance, some fantasy of a bohemian life she'd conjured for herself out of the sepia-hued photographs of Europe she'd seen. Did she imagine herself on city streets, visiting bookstores, frequenting cafés, meeting expats like herself who could not tolerate the narrowness of America? Perhaps the idea of doing things, even the same things, in French seemed less distasteful. So she saved her money and convinced her parents it was just for the summer, just a few months to perfect her French.

But inside her something had hardened—enough to make her believe she could reject everything she had ever known and leave her parents and this country behind forever.

One weekend, word spread on our block that the Mulligans were at war with the Kitteridges, who lived across the street. From where we played in front of the house, Sara, Celia, Celia's little brother Jake, and I watched the Mulligans buzz in and out of their driveway. They stocked weapons, filling water balloons from the spigot in their driveway and piling them in their garage. Then they began scouring the neighborhood in regiments of three and four.

The constant but impersonal harassment the Mulligans bestowed on the rest of us was nothing before the sharply honed hatred they felt for the Kitteridges. The Kitteridges were hopelessly outnumbered. There were only three of them: a boy who seemed to me vastly older, a girl even older than him, and one sad-eyed little seven-year-old known to all of us as "dirty Suzie." It wasn't clear what ignited the war. There may have been an altercation between the oldest Mulligan and the oldest Kitteridge. Michael Kitteridge was a tough, skinny kid, probably only twelve or thirteen years old, with the thinnest instinct for survival. He was gutsy, foolish enough to stand up to the Mulligans alone, perhaps because life had already dealt him blows worse than anything the Mulligans could deliver.

The Mulligans were the Irish Catholic brood of working-class parents. The Kitteridges were hippies, or so we said, because they were sloppy and undisciplined, because they wore strange clothes, because no one ever called them in to dinner, and because their father, thin and no better kempt than they were, sometimes wandered down the street without really going anywhere. In 1972 these differences mattered. Culturally, politically, socially, our family probably fell on the Kitteridge side of the Mulligan-Kitteridge continuum. But with the unerring instinct of children to align with the dominant culture, we sided with the Mulligans.

There was something else. Something everyone knew, but no one talked about. The Kitteridges no longer had a mother. They had had one once—I remembered her messy and huge, with lank brown hair, dressed in gauzy skirts and sandals. Something bad, something very bad, had happened to her, and the shadow of her absence, a dark halo of shame, had attached itself to her children, making them vulnerable to attack.

Late in the afternoon Patrick and Eddie rode their bikes down the block to where we played four-square in front of our house. We scattered as they came, a flurry of long hair, bell-bottom pants, and navy blue Keds. We expected them to ride straight through our game. Instead, Eddie came to a stop, planting his feet on the ground on either side of his pedals. Patrick came up behind him, took the same stance, and glared at us through the opening of the maroon football helmet he wore.

"You're all drafted," Eddie said unceremoniously and then turned to go, motioning for us to follow. Patrick stood still, waiting for us to move, ready to enforce orders. No words passed between the brothers. They had an instinct for coercion.

Among ourselves there must have been a bewildered

exchange of looks. I looked to Sara. Sara and Celia looked to one another. Sara moved first; the rest of us followed. Like an egg from the shell, once the yolk is committed, everything else follows. We walked behind Eddie in silence. Scared. And excited. We'd never played with the Mulligans before. They'd never asked us.

Through the course of the day everyone on the block was bullied into the Mulligan army. No one resisted. The Mulligans had discipline, equipment, and organization on their side; we fell in.

The Mulligans distributed arms: squirt guns, slingshots, rubber bands, and redcaps and firecrackers for noise. They marched us up and down the sidewalk, lining us up by size, me and Jake Jeffers at the rear, chanting, "Two, three, four, hut, we're gonna kick the Kitteridge butt." There was dizzy pleasure in these chants—my guilt at being mean and saying bad words evaporated in the echo of a dozen other voices chanting with me.

The Kitteridges made themselves scarce in the neighborhood; the war was really more of a prolonged hunt. Patrick marched us at a near-run, barking out a rapid "hut, two, three, four, hut." I gripped a metal garbage can lid tight in one hand, my shield, and a majorette baton in the other, my weapon. I kept my eyes on the feet of the boy in front of me and tried to keep pace, hoping we would not find the enemy.

The farther I got from home, the more I felt the gnawing certainty that my mother would not be happy if she saw me. She had very strong opinions about things. Back then she favored the weak over the strong. She was against candy and Barbie and television and Vietnam—fiercely and with disdain for those who did not agree with her. The candy store on the corner, the trading and gathering center of our young lives, where children went to store up reserves for the afternoon play, was directly on our route home from school, but Sara and I were not supposed to go in. And we were absolutely forbidden to watch cartoons on television because they were violent. For my sister and me my mother's rules, aimed as they were at television and candy, at the very heart of childhood, led us to early habits of deception. Sara and I were allied in a daily exploration of the shades of disobedience. Going inside the store ourselves was crossing the line. Standing around outside the candy store while our friends went in was OK. Sneaking the TV on at our house and watching cartoons was definitely bad. But perhaps staying in the room when the TV was on at someone else's house was OK.

I knew we were against the war, maybe even all wars. Vietnam loomed at the edge of my consciousness: a glimpse of helicopters on TV, the sweaty faces of soldiers under hard round hats, the jowly face of the president, whom we did not like, the angry demonstrators, whom we did like. I don't remember the antiwar demonstrations myself, but my father assures me I was there. Each year from 1966 on, my parents marched, pushing the Wonder Chair, carrying first one child, then the next, in crowds 100,000 strong towards Kezar Stadium in the park, where all the rallies ended.

Growing up in Michigan, my father had sworn he'd never

work in a factory or join the army. He told us this so frequently and fervently that it was a core piece of family myth, a coda of his personal identity. For years I had it in my head that my father had "burned his draft card," as if the simple act of burning the card was enough to keep him out of Vietnam. The real story was a bit more complicated. He graduated from college in 1963, and, once his student exemption expired, he was called in for a physical. My parents had been married for two years at the time. They decided to leave the country rather than face the draft. They bought plane tickets for France, but at the eleventh hour, my mother discovered she was pregnant with my sister Sara. My father wrote to his draft board and received a new exemption, which lasted until he was twenty-six, too old to be drafted.

However mangled the story had become in my mind, the message was clear enough: the right thing to do in the face of a draft was to resist.

Here I was three blocks past the street I was not supposed to cross, armed and marching with the strong against the weak. This would not be OK with my mother, not by any stretch.

The Kitteridges stayed out of sight for two days. The Mulligans, bored and frustrated with their undersized and elusive enemy, understood that an army of our size, once armed and fielded, must fight. They divided us into two forces and staged a battle on the sidewalk midway up our block. When the battle began I tossed my water balloon, which plopped down a few feet from me but didn't break. I huddled close to the ground under my metal shield. Balloons exploded onto the sidewalk around me. I heard rubber bands zinging into metal and children shrieking at the cold of water. Dozens of feet fled in all directions. I stayed down. In a matter of minutes, the ammunition was gone, and the sides were advancing, sticks in hand. Sara and Celia came running from the front lines soaked and shaken. Sara pulled me from the ground, and we all went AWOL.

That evening, I leaned against the countertop in the kitchen, watching my mother make meatloaf. She dropped sliced onions, spices, salt, and pepper into a glass bowl. Her fingers curled into the meat, kneading and mixing, growing greasy from the ground beef. She asked about my day. I'd never outright lied to her. Even evasion was new to me. The separation between mother and child needed for deception did not yet exist. Maybe she asked why the ends of my hair were wet. If I told her about the water balloons, that would have led to more questions. In the end, caught up in the excitement again, I told her the whole story: the weapons, the battle, the days of marching, the war.

"Who is this war against?" she asked. My face grew red. I shifted against the counter. She'd honed in on the part of the story I'd been skirting.

"The Kitteridges," I muttered.

"You all ganged up against the Kitteridges?" she asked. In the spotlight of her righteousness I was flooded with shame. I said nothing, working my fingers against the smooth surface of the countertop. She turned back to the meatloaf. "Those poor children," she said. Her hands were still, resting for a moment in the meat. Then she lifted the whole of it from the glass bowl and pressed it into an aluminum loaf pan. She turned back to me, eyes like beams. "Would you like it if somebody treated you that way?"

I could not answer. "We were drafted," I tried to explain, the paltriness of this excuse apparent even to me as I uttered it.

"Drafted?" she said, her eyebrows jumping up.

"If we didn't join, they were going to beat us up."

She offered no sympathy. On matters of principle she did not bend. She placed the meatloaf on the top shelf of the oven. "Then play inside," she said, letting the oven door snap shut.

In the aftermath of the Kitteridge-Mulligan war, my mother cast our family definitively into the hippie-peacenik camp by inviting dirty Suzie over to play with me. "Be nice to her," my mother said. "She doesn't have a mother."

I knew this, and knew I should feel sorry for her. Left on my own, with Suzie in her house and me in mine, I could get to feeling pretty sad for Suzie. But I didn't want her in my house. I feared the censure of the neighborhood. I feared that her motherless condition, along with her famous dirtiness, would rub off on me. She appeared at the front door all the same. Her ratty white blonde hair matted, her face smudged, wearing a plaid skirt, no longer pleated and much too big, and no tights, just skinny bare legs, all cuts, bruises, and yellow down.

Soon enough Suzie and I were sprawled on the living room floor, eyes shut tight as a man's deep voice moved like a ghost across the room. His footsteps came darkly towards us, the sound of stiff man shoes tapping against hardwood floor. He talked about stereo sound. But I didn't listen to what he said. That was the surface. Below that, in the calm insinuation of his voice, was some kind of menace.

Next came the train, a whistle shout off somewhere down the street, and then a rhythmic chug coming closer, louder, stronger. Careening around the last stretch of track, it blew over the couches, over the carpet, and over Suzie and me in a final crescendo of steam and steel. We lay spent, arms and legs spread, prostrate and stunned as the train pulled away. Suzie giggled, a low gurgle. The album, *Stereophonics*, had come with our new, first-on-the-block stereo. I jumped up to place the needle very carefully in the first track, and we listened again.

My mother was upstairs finishing some schoolwork before taking us to the park for a promised paddleboat ride at Stow Lake.

"Let's make a fort," Suzie said, bored finally with the stereophonics. She eyed the fat, leafy green cushions on the two big sofas.

"I don't think my mother will like that," I said. I rarely played in the living room, and knew we were only in here because my mother felt sorry for Suzie.

"Go and ask her."

"I don't want to."

"Come on, don't be such a baby." Suzie, dirty or not, was still a year and a half older than me. I could not say no.

I went slowly up the stairs, taking my time, smoothing the dark wood of the banister with my hand as I went. From upstairs I could hear the music of my mother's electric type-writer—the rapid-fire of the keys, the quick bell at the end of every line, the whoosh of the carriage as it returned. It was an Olivetti, gray, with green keys. Like the piano in the living room, like the sewing machine in the sunroom, it was one of her special things.

That year she'd gone back to school, inspired by the women's movement, freshly minted in 1971, which she greeted with great excitement. My father now says he'd always assumed my mother would go back to school at some point. "She was just so smart, she had to do something." The school she chose was called Lone Mountain College, which seems apt, because for my mother any search for knowledge would have to be a solitary struggle.

As I came into her bedroom I could just barely see the top of her desk, where the pages of her paper were resting lightly at her side. Her fingers were curled down towards the keys, which struck out at the page one at a time, as if each had a life of its own, a path it must follow. She put one arm around my shoulder as I came close to her, and with the other hand she cranked the typewriter wheel several times until the page came loose at the top of the tray. She drew it up and held it in the air for a moment, not reading it, just examining it. The text was crisp, each letter tight where it had scarred the delicate white paper. The typing paper was strange to touch, thin, but rough. If you held it up to the light you could see the word *bond*, embossed in the paper like a secret message. Satisfied, she put the page down and turned to me.

"Mommy, can I build a fort with Suzie in the living room?"

"Oh sweetie, we're going in just a few minutes. Don't let's mess up the living room. OK?" She smiled at me and I said, "OK." It was OK; it was right and simple. We were of one mind, united now against the wild child in the living room. I went down the stairs quickly, ready to lord it over Suzie. It was my house, my mother. No fort.

But Suzie wasn't waiting for me to tell her what to do. She didn't live in the simple world of mother love and obedience. In the living room the naked insides of the couches glared up at me, insides I had seen only on the rare occasions when my mother vacuumed under the cushions.

Suzie was gleefully dragging one last heavy cushion towards the window, where she had already heaped the others.

"She said no," I gasped in genuine horror.

"We'll put them back before she comes," Suzie said, tossing her head and trying to shake her eyes free from her straggly hair while both hands struggled to balance the cushions.

"Come on—help me," she said impatiently. I stood and watched, stunned that I had neither the power nor the words to make her obey.

I couldn't help noticing a small space, a triangle of shade, where one tall cushion leaned against the hard backside of the sofa. It reminded me of the space inside a redwood tree—carved out by fire, shady, triangular, just big enough for a child to crawl into. The cushions were two shades of green, textured and heavy in a paisley, leafy design that caught and reflected the sun where the threads were shiny. Even though it wasn't a fort yet, even though it was still just a pile of pillows, that first shady place was already big enough to crawl into.

Inside, in the half dark, under the forest of green, I asked Suzie, "Where's your mother?"

"Dead," she said, her hoarse voice coming at me out of the darkness. "They found her in the park."

A picture formed in my mind of her mother's large body sprawled among the rocks in the clearing at the top of the path that led to the Tea Garden. It was that kind of place, spooky with tall firs, hidden by the rocks. I imagined the flesh sagging on her arms. Terrible. That she let herself be found like that.

Caught up in these images, I didn't hear my mother's foot-steps on the stairs. Suddenly she was standing in the wide doorway to the living room, hands poised on the high end of her long waist, elbows angled back. I scampered out of my retreat, and the cushions collapsed behind me. The secret place dissolved. My mother was shocked at my direct disobedience. "Laura, what did I tell you?"

Suzie was shy now, her eyes innocently sliding towards me. "We were going to put them back," I stammered. I looked towards Suzie, but I could see no use trying to explain that I had only followed her lead. Weakness of that kind was no excuse. My mother knew no shades of disobedience. No Stow Lake, no paddleboat.

Out of favor, I slunk to my room. Suzie, to my amazement, reverted to her simpering. Rather than punishing her or send-ing her away, my mother decided to give her a bath. From my bedroom I listened to the water running into the tub and their light voices. I had no sympathy for Suzie now. She wasn't even going to be dirty after the bath. Once she was clean—once her yellow hair was washed and shiny—she would look like the blonde girl on the baby shampoo bottle. I rocked Big Baby, my oversized baby doll, in my arms. She was about two feet long, with stiff plastic legs and arms, and a plush, soft torso. I cried into her pink belly.

Afterwards my mother took Suzie into her bedroom and helped Suzie write a letter to her aunt in Manteca. A few months later, Suzie and her brother and sister went to live with this aunt. Suzie's mother had overdosed in the park, and her father, from grief or drugs, was unstable. The letter my mother helped Suzie write may have been the bridge that got her from her father's house to a more stable life. I didn't know or care about those things then. All I knew was that my mother let Suzie use the typewriter, something not even Sara was allowed to do.

Chapter Three

IN THE SUMMER OF 1972, the summer of the Watergate break-in, the summer the last U.S. ground troops left Vietnam, the summer the United States dropped 125,000 tons of bombs on North Vietnam, my father decided to take our family on a three-month trek across America. For weeks, he sat at the dining room table in the evenings with road maps spread before him, figuring travel times and mileage. He marked off sights to see, parsing out the weeks between national parks and visits to family in Michigan, Illinois, and Colorado. He traced our proposed route on a large nationwide map. My mother was too distracted to help with the planning, but in red magic marker she circled Livingston, Montana, because the psychic Edgar Cayce had designated that town as a safe zone, away from the coming apocalypse he predicted for the coasts, and she wanted to see it.

The day we were to leave on what we called "the big trip," I walked home from kindergarten with Sara, giddy with excitement. My father was out front hooking our Oldsmobile to our brand-new Airstream trailer. I stopped to watch, and he let me hold the tools. He knelt at the rear of the car, struggling to fit the iron ball at the back of the station wagon to the metal hitch that extended from the trailer.

I was in love with the Airstream. I loved everything about it—the shiny exterior, the clever use of space inside, the tiny triangular sink in the bathroom, the fact that I got to share a bed with my older sister. There was a tininess about it, an insubstantiality to the walls and doors that put me in mind of dollhouses. I liked the idea of all of us being enclosed in that tight space, of traveling with our beds in tow.

My father muttered curses under his breath from the ground where he lay, trying to force the ball into the hitch of the trailer. The air around us grew thick with frustration, and I began to regret that I had stopped to help. But I was holding the tools now, so I could not slip away.

Most of the mechanical jobs my father did around the house were accompanied by this cussedness. When he had to cut the trunk of the Christmas tree to fit into the stand, when he got under the sink in the kitchen, when he put chains on the tires in a snowstorm—anytime he lay down on the ground in labor, his head hidden from sight—there was this dangerous, angry cussedness. It never occurred to me to question his competence in mechanical matters. He seemed handy and capable to me. He was much handier, for instance, than my mother, handier than my sisters and me.

In fact, he wasn't all that good at chores like these—an old sore spot. He came from a family of men who worked with their hands. Using his head had taken him far, out of Michigan, away from a factory job, but as a kid being smart had never cut it with his "old man." Every time he found himself fighting a wrench, he must have felt his own father watching.

My father grew up in a small town just outside Flint, Michigan, the sixth of seven children in an Irish Catholic family. His father worked on the assembly line at General Motors for forty-five years, in the heyday, before the plant closures, before Flint had a 25 percent unemployment rate. Three of my father's classmates in his graduating class of twenty at St. Mary's High School were his first cousins. You had two choices after getting out of high school in Flint: join the army or work in the factory. Having sworn never to do either (as my father tells anyone who asks), he left Michigan the day after he graduated from high school.

He headed to California, where he lived for a time with his older sister, Joan, who was married and settled in a brand-new suburb of Orange County. Joan held the distinction of being the first person from St. Mary's to graduate from college. My father would become the second.

He met Joe Keith—who would become his closest friend of more than forty years—at the community college where they were both working their way to better things. Joe was a few years older than my father, but from a similar background: Irish Catholic, small town, working class. Substitute the steel mills of western Pennsylvania for the car factories of Flint, and the landscapes of their childhoods were the same.

Joe paid his way by working as a carpenter. My father, better with his head than his hands, landed a job selling pots and pans on commission door-to-door. Sometimes Joe worked with him, and the two of them traveled through small, dusty towns in California's Central Valley and on out through Nevada. They sought out young, just-married couples or—the most fertile ground of all—single women building hope chests. My father's routine: when he got to a new town he'd stand alone, look-ing befuddled, on the sidewalk of the main street. Inevitably, a young woman would approach him and ask if he needed help. With one hand going nervously to the corner of his horn-rimmed glasses, he would explain that, yes, perhaps she could help him. He had this job, you see—he was in town to show household items to single women who were employed and might be interested in making purchases. Perhaps she could put him in touch with such women, perhaps invite a group of her friends for a demonstration? This same approach—same story, same nervous touch to the glasses—worked on female bank tellers and drugstore clerks as well. It worked so well, in fact, that within a few hours he and Joe would have names, phone numbers, and appointments for the day. They moved fast, though, getting in and out of town as quickly as possible because, although my father assures me the business was on the up and up, local sheriffs did not look kindly on out-of-town salesmen.

"They were very good pans," he is always quick to add now

whenever he recalls those days. "You couldn't get pans like that in the stores back then. Not at that price." Quality aside, some combination of charm, audacity, good looks, and an earnest belief in his product made my father a phenomenally good salesman. After just eighteen months on the job, he was the top Vitacraft Cookware salesman in the country. He was twenty years old and had just finished two years of junior college. Vitacraft rewarded his outstanding sales with a down payment on a new Cadillac. Cars didn't interest him much by then; he'd seen plenty of Cadillacs in Flint. He used the money to buy two one-way plane tickets to New York instead. In the fall of 1960, he and Joe boarded the *Queen Elizabeth II* to Europe, retracing my mother and Mary's trip of five months earlier.

Standing next to the Airstream listening to my father curse, I did my best to compensate by holding the tools well, trying to guess which screwdriver he would need before he asked. When my father finally latched the trailer to the car, I followed him into the house. We weren't in a talking mood anymore. My mother was in the kitchen pulling things from the refrigerator: Miracle Whip, mustard, bologna, packages of individually wrapped yellow cheese, and grape juice. My father urged her to finish loading the cooler so he could put it in the car.

My mother did not like to be rushed. Like a large rock in a stream, time flowed unevenly around her. She never knew where it went. She got up late, stayed up late, and liked eating dinner late. She kept people waiting for hours. Having three small children didn't help. Three pairs of shoes, three pairs of socks, all that hair to be brushed, so many barrettes to be found. My sisters and I functioned on her time. We could go no faster than she did. We skulked into church after the singing had already begun. We slipped behind our desks at school in the middle of the Pledge of Allegiance. We were accustomed, but not immune, to the disgusted looks of harried receptionists in doctors' offices when we showed up forty-five minutes late for appointments. Every time we flew to Michigan or Colorado to visit family, the trip to the airport was a nail-biter, with the very real possibility that we would miss our flight. We didn't know there was any other way to live.

My father, though not punctual by normal standards, always knew what time it was. He didn't wear a watch, but he knew. Testing him was a game we never grew tired of. Coming home from an all-day hike, I'd run to the clock in the kitchen to ask him what time it was. Walking back to the car after going out to dinner, we'd make him guess the time. He'd pause for just a moment, then say in his most cocky voice, "Oh it's about ten of nine," or, "It's six twenty, six twenty-five." And always, the clock on the dashboard would be within five minutes of the time he gave.

Before my mother's engulfing lateness he was powerless. He wielded his anger, his best, his only weapon against her, as the thing most likely to "get this show on the road."

As it turns out, even the first time they met, my father had to wait for my mother, although "lying in wait" is a better description of what really happened. It wasn't fate, or even a coincidence, that the door on the landing of their Paris hotel was blocking my mother's path that evening.

"Russ had spotted your mother and Mary earlier," Joe tells me. "He left the door open all afternoon, just waiting for them to come down."

Over the years, I've had this story from my mother, my father, and Joe. The basic facts are the same, but the tone and emphasis shifts, depending on who is telling the tale. My father would never use a word like *fate*, nor would Joe, for that matter. Joe recalls my mother and Mary as a dramatic, stylish pair in short skirts and long black coats. He and my father were, he admits, on the make. They'd been concentrating primarily on European women. More fertile soil. My mother and Mary were not good prospects. "Two schoolteachers from Chicago," says Joe with a smirk. "No chance." But still.

When my father heard the women's heels on the stairs, he would have had time to smooth down his hair, perhaps even pick up a book, and arrange himself on the bed. When my mother peeked around the doorframe—dark hair followed by bright eyes—and their eyes met, as he registered the first charge of attraction, he didn't even have to feign surprise. And she fell weightlessly into the trap.

With the two women standing, my mother resolutely inside, Mary hesitating at the door, they all exchanged names and the regional information that pegged them to home. Michigan, Illinois, western Pennsylvania—they were all from the stolid industrial North.

In a quick aside, or just by some well-greased signal, Joe and my father agreed to pair my mother with Joe and Mary with my father. Mary was tall and Joe was not, so that was that. But as they walked through the Latin Quarter, my mother and father strayed together to the edge of the sidewalk. They fell in step and began to talk.

I think the impression my mother made on my father that night and on Joe, for that matter, stayed in place for years: bold, sophisticated, beautiful, knowledgeable, game for adventure. She knew her way around Paris. She took my father and Joe to a *foyer des étudiants* for a state-subsidized dinner. Students jammed the tables: French, American, Arab, immigrants from the disintegrating French Empire. The war in Algeria was raging full force. The student foyers were alive with talk of it, and served as a staging ground for the roiling protests that rocked the streets of Paris almost every day.

In the weeks that followed, they formed a foursome and then a threesome. Joe says my mother was disappointed that no romance ever developed between Joe and Mary. But Mary, it seems, could not keep pace with the other three. Joe vividly remembers my mother, fluent in French, stopping strangers on the street to ask questions: What was going on? Who were the protesters? What were the police doing? Where was the best café? Then leading them on.

Once the three of them were running full force from the charging gendarmes, amid tear gas, batons, and rock-throwing students. The heel of my mother's pump caught in a gutter. All three of them squatted down in the street, huddled around my mother, tugging until the shoe came loose. My father and Joe pulled my mother to her feet. They set off running again.

They never knew exactly who was protesting what. There were the students, there were the right-wing French Algerians who waged their campaign of terror in Paris, and then there were the police, who were shockingly brutal to everyone. For my parents it was all new. The scenes in the streets were thrilling and horrifying. Still, it wasn't their country; it wasn't their cause. Mostly they ran.

Among themselves, they spent long nights in conversation. I can see my mother, an inveterate night owl, seated between Joe and my father holding forth with a glass of red wine in her hand, her legs crossed neatly under the table. All of them lean forward in ardent conversation. My mother had a keen interest in politics. She followed the events of the civil rights movement closely. She worried intensely about the bomb. Both Joe and my father admit that she educated them. I imagine her doubly animated in the presence of such an eager male audience.

When the sun came up and they were still out, they walked across the river to Les Halles to eat onion soup and thick bread with the morning workers. Joe says, without qualification, "Those were happy times."

In early 1961, Joe heard he had a letter from his draft board waiting for him at home. My mother, he recalls, was full of schemes to keep him out of the army. "Sally offered to shoot me in the foot herself." He declined her offer and went home to join the reserves rather than wait and be drafted.

To force my mother home, my grandfather had stopped

sending money. She was dead broke and dependent on my father to pay the bills. Still, they traveled to Munich, Berlin, Amsterdam, and then Brussels. They wrote letters to Joe describing their escapades: car trouble and car accidents, tight money, angry landlords "jabbering" in languages they didn't understand. In one letter, my mother tells how she had to bring the car around to the front of a restaurant for a fast getaway, while my father gave the police the slip. In Munich, they lived for two weeks on eight dollars, avoiding the landlady, eating every meal at an automat that took their francs for marks, before money finally arrived, wired by my father's sister from the States. She closes with, "In spite of our troubles, we're getting along very well and having a good time. Even after this long, we still love each other madly so we don't care if the whole world is against us." Only she crossed out *madly*.

Maybe it was then, just as she put those words on paper, that the idea became fixed in her head: the world was against them, but their love was a powerful, protective force—not a novel idea, but it anchored her existence for the next ten years.

My father had always planned to go back—back to college, back to southern California, back to America. My mother was in deep enough to let him buy tickets home for both of them. They shared a stateroom, choosing the French line because the French were less particular about marital status than the British. According to my father, despite the comfort and the luxury of the *Normandie*, the trip home wasn't easy. My mother was nauseated the whole time and depressed about returning to the States. To their mutual shock, she had a miscarriage midway through the voyage. Neither had known she was pregnant.

When they separated in New York, nothing was resolved between them. My father alludes darkly to her "hysteria" in the hotel room before they parted. "I knew something was not right," he says. In hindsight, he sees this as the flashing red light he chose to ignore. He could have gotten out right then, but he didn't. He was already hooked.

I can't judge the quality of her hysteria, but I am struck by two things. The ocean voyage from Europe took four days. When they parted in New York, she'd just had a miscarriage, with the attendant crash in hormones that followed. My father may have underestimated the impact on my mother, for whom pregnancy and childbirth caused profound mood swings. Plus, she was back in the United States, where she'd dreaded returning. She had no plans of her own and no firm commitment from my father. Freewheeling it in Europe was one thing, but her family back in Illinois wasn't going to understand anything short of a ring. Maybe a little hysteria was in order.

She went home to Illinois, my father to California. A few months later, she visited him in San Diego, where he was then in school. She ended up staying, moving in, and six months later, in a midweek civil ceremony, they were married.

Looking back, my father now says my mother was depressed when they met in Paris. Mushroom clouds haunted her dreams, and she felt an almost irrational sense of despair over returning to the United States. His account doesn't square with Joe's unqualified "happy times." I don't doubt my father, but I can't help wondering how much the shadow of the intervening years now darkens his memories of her.

All my informants agree on one thing: My parents were deeply in love. Even my father does not stint on this. He's told me that for years, long after they were married, when they went out together, he and my mother were so intent upon one another, so visibly in love, that people would come over and buy them drinks.

By the summer of 1972, nobody was buying my parents drinks anymore. I didn't know it, but by then my father was near the end of his wits, and my mother was already considerably beyond hers.

On the day we left, I was upstairs dressing my favorite doll, Big Baby, when I heard a loud crash and then my father's "mother-fucking hell." I ran down to the first floor and peered down the entryway steps that led to the front door. My father was crouched on the stairs where he had fallen. The tightly packed cooler he'd dropped had skidded down the stairs and slammed into the front door.

My mother appeared at my side, a basket of laundry in her arms. It was three o'clock in the afternoon. We had planned to leave at one. My father stood up, leaning forward to favor his left ankle. "Oh, for Christ's sake, Sally, are you going to wash everything in the house? If you don't quit, we won't get out of here until tomorrow." This was not hyperbole. We had, on more than one occasion, begun packing the car one afternoon, only to finally pull out of the driveway the next morning.

"Help me with the cooler," he said. "Then get the kids in the goddamn car and let's go."

His anger could still, at times, move her. She left the laundry basket on the step, and went, lifting one handle of the cooler with him. "This thing is heavy as hell," my father said, by way of explanation.

My mother rushed back upstairs and called for us. "Come on girls, let's go." She herded the three of us before her, down the two flights of stairs, and then hustled us into the back seat. My father was sitting in the driver's seat, looking straight ahead. As she opened the passenger door and started to get in, she turned to look at him, then said, "Oh, wait just a sec," and ran back into the house. This gave my father the opportunity to expel more angry air. She returned a few long silent minutes later with the laundry basket piled high, wet and dry clothes mixed together. We all turned to watch as she shoved the basket in through the small side door of the trailer. Then she climbed into her place on the front bench seat of the station wagon.

My father drove in silence. He took the turns too hard so the trailer careened dangerously around the corners. We were quiet, held in the tension of his anger. Like being jinxed. Until he said the word, we could not speak.

Sara and I began a surreptitious game of rock, paper, scissors across Amy's lap in the back seat. We foreshortened and controlled our movements, keeping our arms below the seat so my father wouldn't catch sight of us in the rearview mirror having fun. I squinted and watched Sara's eyes on each round, trying to read her mind. Sometimes, just often enough to feed my faith, it worked. Amy, not yet three, followed the steady motions of our hands with her eyes. Sara and I kept score with the fingers of our free hands. Win or lose, we kept a tight silence.

By the time we got on the Bay Bridge, my father's anger had begun to dissipate. He tried grudgingly to win back our favor. "OK, you turkeys, what did you forget?" he asked. "Everybody got their swimsuits? Blankies? Dolls?" My stomach clenched as I remembered Big Baby sitting on my bed, where I had left her when the cooler crashed.

"Big Baby," I whispered, mostly to my mother. There was no place to turn around on the Bay Bridge. I knew this. My mother turned to look at me, to judge my level of despair. Then she turned towards my father. "Russ?" she said, testing the waters.

"We're not going back." He steeled himself against the shivering wave of sympathy that moved between the four of us, fearing it would swamp the car, reverse our momentum, stop the trailer, turn this whole trip around.

My mother looked back at me again, her eyebrows locked down in concern. I knew that if it were up to her, we'd go back. I hoped she would fight for me.

She said, more slowly now, trying to sound sensible, "Russ, couldn't we just turn around at Treasure Island and go back real fast?" Then, after a pause, "It's three months."

"Sally, we're not going back for a doll—for Christ's sake. It's quarter to four. If we go back now we're on this bridge until seven o'clock."

She shot him an angry look, then sat back in her seat. I willed her to speak again, but I knew she'd given up.

Amy flashed a sympathetic look in my direction. A few minutes later my mother turned to me. "Well, pumpkin," she said, "we can buy you another doll in Oregon."

I began to cry. My mother reached back over the seat to pat my hand. I pulled away from her and turned into the door on my side. I would rather cry all the way across America than get another doll. I'd take misery and loyalty over betrayal every time. It was something I already knew about myself.

I leaned on my arms against the window, trying to count the silver rails of the bridge as they flashed by, trying to imagine how long three months was. I cried quietly so as not to rouse my father. I wanted to be able to measure out the days, bit-by-bit, moment-by-moment, so I could know how to survive them. But I couldn't. The silver rails on the bridge blurred together. There was nothing to hold on to. Three months was too big.

Somewhere out there, out past Vacaville, Sara tapped my knee and we began again, silently swinging our fists in time. The words echoed only in our heads. *Row, sham, bow. Rock, paper, scissors.*

Chapter Four

IN THE FRONT SEAT of the station wagon, my mother sat Indian-style, with Pearl S. Buck's *New Living Bible* spread open on her lap. She read in a clear rhythmic voice, "Take your son Isaac, your only son, whom you love, and go to the land of Moriah."

My father drove silently, one hand poised lightly at the bottom of the steering wheel, the other resting on his knee. We'd been in the car all day, on the road between Yellowstone and Glacier national parks. Behind the station wagon the Airstream pitched gently through the curves. My sisters and I were slumped three abreast in the backseat. The long hours in the car, the summer heat, the hum of the engine, the smooth roll of the tires on the highway, and my mother's voice had a hypnotic effect. I leaned against the door of the car. Amy, forever stuck in the middle, leaned up against me. I could tell from the weight of her body that she was sleeping. My body was heavy too, but I was wide-awake, transfixed by the story.

"Abraham rose early in the morning and saddled his ass, and he took with him two of his men and his son Isaac," my mother intoned.

She'd decided to read us the Bible from start to finish, beginning the day we left San Francisco. As we traveled north through the deepening green of Oregon and Washington, then east through Idaho and Montana, the slim white ribbon that marked our place in the huge Bible inched its way through Genesis.

We got as far east as Michigan that summer before my father tacked back west to get us home in time for school in the fall. My mother kept up with the Bible reading even after we got home, stopping two years later just short of Revelation.

At church on Sundays in the hard pew next to my mother, I tried to cleave to the minister's words. The only idea that had really sunk in was that Jesus loved me. The Old Testament was a shock. The language was strange, the morality hard, and this unforgiving God much tougher than anything I'd come up against until then. But the stories held me. From time to time as she read, my mother would pause to explain things to us: what a birthright was and how it could be stolen, what a covenant was and how it could be broken. Some things she could not explain.

"Father, Isaac said, here are the fire and the wood, but where is the young beast for the sacrifice?"

My mother paused for a moment, turned in her seat, and looked back at us. She saw that Amy was sleeping. "Well, that's enough for today," she said, drawing the silk marker down between the pages and closing the book carefully. My father glanced at her. He didn't like the Bible that much. He didn't go to church with us on Sundays anymore. What he liked were car games, racing to see who could find all the letters of the alphabet on road signs, or who could sight the most out-of-state license plates. My mother didn't play. Even packed tight into the station wagon, it was getting so you couldn't be with both of them at the same time.

I sat back in my seat, my mind fumbling over the story. *Poor Isaac.* I shrugged Amy off my shoulder and turned towards the window to watch the open country. Amy, awakened abruptly, turned to me. Her face was crumpled up, eyes beseeching. All she wanted, all she ever wanted, was to lean up against someone to sleep.

I shook my head at her. Pushing her off me with one hand, I silently redrew the line on the seat that marked my territory from hers.

She turned to Sara, "Can I?"

Sara, staring out her own window, shook her head without looking over.

My mother turned around again. "Come up front, baby," she said, holding out her arms. Amy went, headfirst, over the bench seat. I watched her go, too lazy even to reach out and slap her butt as it rose up over the seat.

I retreated into my own territory, holed up against the window, trying to get my head around this story. That God would ask, that Abraham would agree. I turned to look back at the trailer. The two propane tanks at the front of the trailer bobbed upright just behind the hookup. The Airstream's sleek rounded form was reassuring.

On these mountain roads the station wagon couldn't pull the trailer at much more than a crawl. With the Airstream attached to our wood-paneled Oldsmobile station wagon, we were forty-five feet long. Fully loaded, we could do only forty miles an hour, slower through turns. This pace must have been tough for my father, who normally drove in the left lane, weaving right only to pass.

Cars had piled up behind us, so my father pulled into the gravel arc of a turnout to let them pass. A huge RV camper went by. I caught the eyes of a boy about my age, in the high side window. During the three months of our trip I had come to understand the hierarchy of recreational vehicles. I loved our trailer, but I couldn't help envying those RV kids. I thought about how that boy could move around anywhere in back while they were on the road. I imagined him lying in his bed, watching cartoons, eating sugar cereal from the box.

This was not the first time my parents had traveled by trailer. In 1965, as Lyndon Johnson ordered the first combat troops to Vietnam, my parents returned to Europe, not to flee the draft as they'd planned two years earlier, but nevertheless pushed by the war. My father says they went because it didn't feel like a normal time, a time for business as usual. For my mother, no time felt like a time for business as usual. The turmoil of the mid-1960s allowed them to share this sense of crisis for a time. They bought a car and a small house trailer in Germany and traveled like gypsies across Europe for ten months. To me the photos of that trip—of Sara in a bonnet and matching wool coat below the Eiffel Tower, of my mother in black capris holding Sara's hand on the Acropolis—spoke of a more golden, blessed time.

When my parents returned from this second stay in Europe, they moved to the Bay Area, first to Oakland, because they couldn't afford the city, and then finally, triumphantly to San Francisco in 1966, just in time for my birth.

My mother convinced my father to pursue a Ph.D. in history. My father always says now that she was the one who should have pursued the degree; she was the real intellectual. For a couple of years he hacked away on his degree at San Francisco State, selling baby furniture and then real estate on the side to support the family. Around the time Amy was born, he dropped out and went into business full-time. It was obvious to him that selling was what he was really good at, but my mother had a visceral distaste for business. She felt it was beneath my father's talent, and for her it must have echoed her father's decision to leave the ministry to make money.

After her own brief foray in graduate school, my mother's vision had turned entirely inward. She cut off ties with most of her old friends, refusing to see people, refusing even to leave the house much. She started reading Edgar Cayce, whose blend of Christianity, prophecy, and belief in reincarnation dovetailed neatly with her own background and preoccupations. Cayce was a Baptist preacher from a small town in the South, not unlike my mother's father. He died in 1940, but he was in many ways the father of the New Age movement. The story of his life, of the 14,000 psychic readings he'd done, and of his complex cosmology was popularized in books written by his family and followers, published in the 1960s. My mother devoured them.

She'd long been attuned to her dreams. Now she looked to them for signs and portents: Should we move to a new house? Should my father buy a building? What schools should my sisters and I attend? Even her diet was dictated by dreams, and she kept eliminating things—no sugar, no meat, no eggs, no onions—until she was down to a few leafy green vegetables, which in the 1970s came in frozen blocks from deep down inside the grocer's freezer.

She'd taken up meditation. And sometimes, she admitted to my father, when she meditated she heard voices. Despite this, she meditated every day, drawn forward into her own terror.

All my mother's interests—the spiritual questing, meditation, macrobiotic diet, mistrust of processed foods—were consistent with the time and place she inhabited. Edgar Cayce's books were on the *New York Times* bestseller lists throughout the late 1960s and 1970s. The very notion of "mental illness" as illness was under attack. Thomas Szasz published *The Myth of Mental Illness* in 1961. R. D. Laing's *The Politics of Experience*, published in 1967, sold six million copies and popularized Laing's view that normalcy was unconscious complicity with a diseased social order. True sanity, he believed, required the dissolution of the socially constructed ego through meditation and spiritual practice. In this view, hallucinations could be seen as an experiential passage—requiring not drugs or incarceration in hospitals but shamanic accompaniment.

I don't know whether either of my parents read these writers. They didn't need to. By 1972 hostility to traditional psychiatry had reached cultural ascendancy, certainly in the borderlands of San Francisco bohemia that my parents inhabited.

Neither of my parents experimented with drugs. My mother had a lifelong aversion, bordering on paranoia, to putting any form of medication into her body. She didn't take aspirin, and as early as 1963, when Sara was born, had insisted on natural childbirth, despite heavy opposition from the doctors. Those battles over childbirth left her with an ongoing suspicion and hostility towards doctors.

My parents may not have taken drugs, but plenty of people around them did. Widespread use of hallucinogens normalized and even romanticized altered mental states. My father recalls seeking advice about my mother from a friend in Berkeley well versed in the transcendental arts. This friend took my mother's hallucinations more or less in stride. "There's a lot of garbage out there in the universe," he told my father. "When you open yourself to it, you take in the bad with the good." Such were the times.

In his gut my father, a natural-born skeptic, knew something was seriously wrong. But he didn't imagine it was permanent. He loved my mother deeply, and he thought he could fix whatever was wrong. She needed to get out of the house; he needed to spend more time with her. He'd made enough money selling real estate to keep us all afloat, so he took the three months off for this trip as an emergency measure, believing that if he could isolate us all in a small space, if he gave my mother his full attention all summer, he could heal the problem that he still could not name.

When we got to Glacier we set up camp. My father unfurled the green and white striped canvas awning from the top of the Airstream. He pulled down the metal stairs that folded out neatly to the ground so we could go in and out the door that swung off the side of the trailer.

My mother sat in a folding chair under the awning, reading a battered copy of Edgar Cayce's *There Is a River*, while my father grilled hamburgers for himself and my sisters and me. We ate on bright yellow plastic camp plates around the fire. We had to have our hamburgers on whole-wheat English muffins—my mother wouldn't buy white bread products like real hamburger buns for us, though she didn't hold the rest of us to her even stricter diet. She joined us around the campfire but ate only her muffin and frozen spinach, which she warmed on the little stove in the trailer.

We sat around the campfire in the evenings, and other men stopped by to talk with my father. He joined in the easy sociability of those camps. The men talked routes and campgrounds: where you could get a hookup, where you couldn't; Airstreams versus RVs. Here in Glacier, they talked about grizzly bears.

"This," one of the men said, "is what a grizzly does to an Airstream." He held up a beer can and crushed it in his hand.

Later, inside the trailer, my sisters and I knelt with my mother at the side of the bed Sara and I shared. We rattled off our lists of god blesses: grandma and grandpa, Sara and Amy, Mommy and Daddy. Together, we recited the Lord's Prayer. We started strong—*Our Father who art in heaven*—Sara and me trailing just behind my mother, missing a word here or there. Amy stumbled, pouncing on an occasional familiar word like someone hopping from stone to stone to cross a stream. The prayer rose and fell around us, from *kingdom come*, to *daily bread*, to *forgive us our sins*, to *forever and ever* until we all landed firmly on *Amen*. When we rose to go to bed, the crisscross pattern of the aluminum floor was etched into our knees.

Sara and I slept on a cushioned bunk about three feet wide, with barely enough wiggle room for both of us. Amy slept directly over our heads in a sling bed, which, when she was in it, hung down so low that it was nearly impossible to resist reaching up and tickling or poking her through the supple pleather of her hammock. My parents slept up front, in a bed that folded out over the table and built-in bench where we sometimes ate.

Lying in bed, I listened to Sara's even breathing and the intermittent murmur of my parent's voices from the fire outside. The rangers drove through the campground. The lights of their truck lit up the inside of the trailer, momentarily revealing the curved outline of the low ceiling. I could see the smooth single shell of aluminum, the thick rivets pressed into the metal. The light passed on.

I heard the rattle of the door handle and caught the sharp

smell of kerosene as my parents came inside with the lantern. They whispered while they settled into bed. Then the yellow light dimmed slowly as my father turned the key on the lantern's wick. I slept safe in the knowledge that everyone was close by, cradled in the shell of the Airstream.

In the morning I woke, sleepy, with tangled hair. The door of the trailer swung open and I stepped out into cold air, the scent of pine, and surely—had I raised my eyes—mountains. But all I remember is the stubbly field near the trailer where we played kickball every afternoon, giving way to taller grass, and then in the distance the long log building where the bathrooms and showers were, men on one side, women on the other. I followed my mother to the bathroom, clutching my toothbrush in my hand, in the biting air. The water, which never heated up in those places, numbed my fingers as I washed my hands. My mother rubbed my face with a washcloth, made rough by the cold, wiping the sleep from my eyes.

We traveled cross-country for three months that summer, camping in KOAs and national parks, visiting family "back east," which was really just the far end of the Midwest. We moved through breathtaking country. Only I don't remember it. What I remember is the rhythm of the days: the inside of the car, the sound of my mother's voice, the close air of the trailer, the pine scent of the national parks, the subtle bouncing from one parent to the other that had already begun.

My father claims that one morning we woke to find long scratch marks across the door of the trailer, the mark of the bears that stalked the collective imagination of the camp-grounds. I have no memory of that either.

What I do have is a photo of my sisters and myself sitting with my mother on the edge of a raft on the Snake River in Wyoming. I'm leaning my head against my mother's shoulder. Sara is in profile, her teeth already jutting forward in an overbite. Amy, just three years old, tucked under my mother's arm, is smiling straight into the camera. My mother wears round, John Lennon sunglasses. She's very thin, in a white cotton sweater that looks too heavy for summer, a crocheted beret, and a very large blue cross, edged in gold, hanging at her throat. She's half smiling, looking at the camera, but the sunglasses obscure her gaze. My sisters and I have dark green life jackets strapped on over our T-shirts. My mother isn't wearing a life jacket. The three of us are tethered to her. She is tethered to nothing.

At Glacier my father perfected the kickball round robin he had devised so Sara, Amy, and I could play an evenly matched game. Standing in the middle of the diamond we had drawn in the stubby grass, my father pitched the rubber ball in a modulated bowl. It bounced unevenly and then rolled straight into home. I stood back to get a running start, then blasted the ball to the left. My father dove for the ball, alive with the limitless energy that physical exertion and competition unleashed in him, caught it on the bounce, righted himself, shifted directions, and beat me to first base.

My third time up, I kicked a hard line drive that he couldn't reach. He turned to the side, put his hands on his hips, let out a low whistle as it passed, and said, "Nice kick, Laura." I ran the bases happy, his praise the only prize that mattered.

After my home run, I went into the trailer to pee. I found my mother seated with her legs crossed under her on the flat space of my parents' foldaway bed. She sat up straight, her head almost reaching the low ceiling of the trailer. Her eyes were closed and she was still. The trailer hugged the summer heat, incubating the morning, but she didn't seem to mind.

I was quiet because I knew I wasn't supposed to bother her when she was meditating. As I came up the stairs she opened her eyes.

"How do you meditate?" I asked.

"You try to feel your breath and make every thought leave your head," she said. "You think nothing. That's the hard part."

I wanted to try, so she let me climb up next to her on the bed. I crossed my legs and placed my hands very gently, palms up, on my knees as she did. I touched my thumbs to my middle fingers like the fat Buddha in the park. I closed my eyes and thought, "Nothing, nothing, nothing." That part was easy.

I sat very still and tried to feel the stream of air flow in and out of my body. I felt nothing. I raised one hand quickly to my mouth. No air. I opened my eyes and looked over at my mother. She was far away. Her eyelids rested over her eyes as gently and calmly as her hands rested on her knees. Her chest rose and fell. Her breasts lifted the heavy gold cross she wore, then let it drop again. I looked down at my own chest and saw nothing. No breasts, no movement, no breath.

Outside I heard the soft punt of the ball as Sara kicked it, then the scramble of her feet over gravel. I was up next but decided to let my turn pass.

I closed my eyes again, clamping them down this time, thinking, "Breathe, breathe, breathe." Searching for air, I came up with nothing.

A long time passed. The small refrigerator next to the bed hummed. A fly searched the screen of the window behind my head for an opening. It landed and crawled in silence for a moment, then lifted off and buzzed again. Behind the buzzing, low and constant, was the hum of the gnats that hovered at the screen. I had to pee.

My mother opened her eyes.

"I can't feel my breath," I said.

She nodded. "It takes a lot of practice. Years and years." I knew she had missed my point, but I didn't press.

In the days that followed, as we began the slow trek home, I watched myself. I must be breathing all the time, I reasoned. Maybe it was just when I thought about it that I stopped. In the backseat of the station wagon, turning towards the window so my sisters would not see, I quickly drew my hand to my mouth, to catch the breath before it fled. Nothing. Standing next to the trailer, I would sneak a sideways glance at my own reflection, murky in the aluminum surface of the Airstream. It was always the same. My chest didn't move. Even holding a hand in front of my mouth and counting to sixty, I couldn't flush myself out.

By now, alive but not breathing, I was as intrigued as I was worried. The inescapable conclusion was that I was not like other people. Perhaps it was all the Bible stories, the miracles and chosen ones. Being different from other people struck me as a good thing, possibly even holy.

I took a chance and told Sara. "I don't think I breathe." I knew as soon as the words were out of my mouth that I sounded like a dope.

"You don't have to think, dumdum, you just do it. If you didn't, you'd be dead."

Out loud I knew she was right. Inside I wasn't convinced. I went on testing, but kept the results to myself. Half terror, half visions of grandeur—as we made our way back to California, I too waited and watched for more signs.

When we got home Big Baby was waiting there for me, lying on my bed just where I'd left her. Only she seemed like a stranger to me. A few months later we moved to a new apartment, and I lost track of Big Baby. Much later, I found her again, naked and abandoned at the bottom of a cardboard box in a closet. The sight of her nearly broke me. I sobbed uncontrollably into her soft belly, stricken, not because I'd lost her, but because I'd forsaken her.

Chapter Five

OUR NEW APARTMENT was on West Clay Park—a three-block cul-de-sac that sloped down 24th Avenue across two blocks lined with beautiful homes, each one unique, with trees and flowering plants in the front yards. The street turned and came back up 22nd Avenue to Lake Street. The neighborhood was more affluent than our old one. We were already strange here: the only kids who lived in an apartment building and the only ones who went to public school. The apartment was much smaller than the old house had been—but because we owned the whole building, it was a step up in the world. There were six units in all, occupied by people who shared walls and ceiling with us. Buying this building was pure audacity on my father's part. He leveraged everything else we had, our house on 12th Avenue and his shares in another building downtown. When you came down to it, all we had amounted to debt, which is how real estate in California works: you turn a little debt into a lot of debt, and then you wait for everything to appreciate.

I saw the apartment for the first time the day before we moved in. It was clear of furniture. Sky blue wall-to-wall carpet had just been laid down from the long front hallway, straight through the living room all the way to the bay windows that looked out on the Golden Gate Bridge. While my parents poked around, making sure the windows opened and closed after the new paint job, Sara and I ran up and down the track, arms out from our sides, soaring through the open space of our new pad in our thin-soled blue Keds. We ran at full speed, stopping dangerously just short of the full-length windows each time, leaving our fingerprints on the panes.

Bliss like this had its price. Later it was discovered that one or both of us had stepped in dog shit and trailed it up and down, again and again across the brand-new carpets. I don't know for sure if it was Sara, or me, or both of us—but she took the blame and I slipped through unnoticed, a pattern that would repeat. The carpets had to be shampooed—my father was very angry. The apartment was already soiled.

We had a spectacular view of the Golden Gate Bridge, and we would gather for sunsets in the living room. We watched the reflective red drama light up the Bay, then deepen down into night. Sometimes in the middle of the day, my father would call, "Hey, girls, come look at this." We'd run to his side to see a tanker, a barge, or, rarest of all, a cruise ship, all lit up, gliding through the Golden Gate. My father stood leaning against the tall window frame. We waited for the boats to pass under the bridge. When my sisters and I tired of the hushed feeling, we slipped back to our games. My father would stay there, his right arm raised against the window frame, his left hip jutting out to the side, gazing after those ships until they reached the open sea.

One evening as we sat at the dinner table, Sara raised her fork to me in a silent challenge. I smiled my assent and piled as large a hunk of steak as I thought I could manage onto my fork. We counted in our heads, punching our forks forward in the air to synchronize our signals: *On your marks, get set, go.* Then we settled in for a long, slow chew. This was not a race; it was an endurance match. Whoever chewed longest without laughing won. I stood a fair chance of beating my older sister at this game.

Swiss steak was one of my mother's mainstay meals. I loved it. I loved the taste of everything stewed together, tomatoes, green peppers, onions, and the meat itself, which was both tender and stringy, requiring long chewing. Our game was born at a moment, long ago, when Sara and I caught each other's eye across the table and giggled at the absurdity of so much chewing.

As I chewed, I glanced over at my mother to see if she was watching us, if she was annoyed. She was gazing out the window over my father's shoulder. Her eyes looked very blue against the pallor of her skin. I leaned forward to see what she saw. The top of one orange tower of the Golden Gate Bridge peered through the fog. I swallowed without thinking, and then, realizing what I had done, looked up to see Sara's eyes gleaming with victory. A smile was slowly growing around her mouth as her chewing came to a stop. Not wanting her to gloat for long, I quickly forked another piece of meat, and we began again.

My family sat around the long oval table where we ate each night with my mother at the head, near the swinging kitchen door, and my father at the other end, his back to the tall windows that looked out to the bridge. Sara, Amy, and I were spread between them. Though we had been in this apartment for over six months, it still felt strange to me, as if the table, the high-backed chairs, the room itself, demanded more of us at ages three, six, and nine than my sisters and I could possibly manage.

Tonight we were eating early, while the sun set, so my father could resume his vigil in front of the television when we finished. The images on the screen never changed—a permanent specter of old men hunched over microphones. The drone of their voices, formal, but always with a barely veiled indignation, filled the apartment every night. Watergate. I had never seen anything as joyless, yet my father relished it. He watched with the bitter glee of one who is finally vindicated, though the world must crumble in order for him to be right.

Sometimes I would sit on the arm of his chair, trying to be companionable. "Who's winning, Daddy?" I'd ask. He'd glance over at me, eyes fixing on my face for just a second, and say, "I think we are, sweetie. I think we are." Then his eyes would shift back to the television screen, rapt.

At the dinner table, as Sara and I began another round of chewing, my father told my mother the story of his day. The conversation floated over my head, and I heard only the comforting refrain, rhythmic and steady, the "he says," "and then I say," "and then he says to me" that marked these stories of verbal sparring, of the deal making and deal breaking that were my father's business.

Sara and I were nearing the end of a particularly long bout. Eyes locked together, chewing with exaggerated strain, we struggled to stave off giggles. On the periphery of my vision, I saw Amy, her chin just clearing the plate in front of her, sitting between Sara and my mother. She fidgeted in her chair, rolled her eyes up under her lids, and twisted her face to try and break my concentration. I held Sara's gaze without wavering.

My jaw was sore from chewing. I held one last shred of meat, all the taste chewed out of it, in my mouth, when Sara finally cracked a smile. We both dissolved in giggles, heads coming down to the table in unison.

Almost as soon as we began to laugh, I realized the laughter was wrong. The current of the conversation above me had shifted. My mother was no longer listening passively. Her attention, which wandered so often these days, had caught on something. She was roused, and when she was roused I was roused too, vigilant, careful, watchful. I straightened in my seat.

My mother shot sharp questions at my father. "Who's Hawkins? I've never heard you talk about him before."

"He's just a guy, Sally. A guy in business," my father said.

"Well, he doesn't sound like a very good guy."

"I don't know if he is good or not, Sally. I'm just selling him some property."

"Well, I don't think you should work with him," she said, her voice rushed and rising to a pitched finality. "I don't think you should work with him at all."

"Oh, for crying out loud, Sally," my father exploded. "This is real estate. You don't choose who you work with." He stabbed his fork into his steak, ratcheting up the anger despite himself, then fell silent.

He chewed hard as he ate, so that his sideburns jumped when his jaw clenched. My mother watched him. Her face was still, and she had stopped eating. I tried to catch Sara's eyes across the table, but they flickered past mine and fixed instead on my father.

"Well, I don't want you to work with him," my mother said, her head shaking slightly but rapidly back and forth. "There's something wrong about him."

My father swallowed hard. "Sally, you don't know him," he said.

"I don't need to know him," she said slowly. "I know."

I arranged my peas across my plate with my fork. The fork was heavy in my hand, weighty silver, but dull and tarnished. The peas were a vivid green against the white plate. They rolled and bounced as I moved them. The almost perfect spheres created patterns on the plate, choosing a twin, forming a triad, then shifting alignments again.

My father sat back in his chair, his shoulders slumped down

slightly. He spoke sharply, down into his food. "That's great, Sal. That's just great." He looked straight up at her again. "I'm not going to drop a client every time you get a bad feeling or have a goddamn bad dream. Somebody's got to earn some money around here."

I turned towards my mother. The table was silent, except for the sounds of my father eating. His fork clanked against his plate. My mother was perfectly still, her delicate features stiff, all her concentration fixed on my father.

I pushed a few peas onto my knife, and glanced back up at my mother, trying to catch her eye. This was a cue for her, an old, familiar one. I wanted her to smile and recite for me, "I eat my peas with honey. I've done it all my life. It makes my peas taste funny, but it keeps them on my knife." She didn't move.

"Sally, can't we just finish eating our dinner?" my father said, still making a great show of eating his own steak.

My mother didn't move, didn't speak. I watched her, but her eyes were glued on him. Because she was so thin, her cheekbones stood out. Her mouth was closed, but the outline of her teeth showed under her upper lip. There was a hardness on her face that I didn't recognize. Her hands, in fists, rested on either side of her plate. She gripped her fork in her right hand.

Sara, sitting next to my father, brought her food slowly to her mouth. Her straight black hair had fallen forward on both sides of her face, making a veil that hid her eyes from mine. She took very small bites, chewed them with care, then swallowed.

My father broke first. Looking up again to face my mother's cold stare, he quickly put both his hands against the edge of the curved table and pushed his chair back. "I've had enough," he said.

She rose with him, fast and sudden, leaning into the table as if to reach out and restrain him. In one deft movement, her body charged with energy, she raised her fist in the air and sent the heavy fork straight at my father.

For just a split second, I met Sara's eyes in horror as we both tracked the path of the fork. My father, thin and agile, shifted his weight back just in time, almost losing his balance, then catching himself on the arm of the chair. The fork just missed him. It slammed into the china cabinet behind him, the one that held my mother's cut glass collection. The thin glass of the cabinet door shattered. I sat very still, my hands gripping the sides of my chair, blinking at the long, sharp, curved shards of glass that lay on the hardwood floor.

Afterwards, we all sat in the living room in a silence punctuated by my mother's sobs. She was huddled in one of the big wing chairs, her knees pulled up close to her chest, her arms wrapped tightly around her knees, her head down. My father sat on the green couch leaning forward, elbows jammed into his knees, looking down at the floor. Then his eyes fell on me. I sat on the floor with my legs folded under me, tracing the lines in the throw rug with one finger. This rug had come with us from our old house on 12th Avenue; it was a color my mother called midnight blue. The pattern etched in the carpet formed a huge, circular maze that extended across the room. I had been tracing these lines as long as I could remember. I would begin at the outer edge of the circle, keeping my forefinger nestled in the track. When I butted up against a dead end, I reversed myself, retracing my route until I found an open path. Slowly, I wound my way into the center.

"Laura, go give your mother a hug," my father said quietly, gesturing towards her with his head.

A loud sob wracked the room. I looked at my father doubtfully. I was not ready to forgive her, much less touch her. Her sobbing made her terrible and strange. I could not understand why he felt sorry for her, why he, her target, was ready to forgive—or why he sent me to comfort her.

He nodded at me again, more firmly this time. Under his gaze, I slowly lifted myself up off the rug and went to my mother. I put my fingertips on her shoulders and began to give her a tentative hug. She lifted her head and raised her bloodshot eyes to me. I started to cry. She opened up her lap and drew me in. She keened back and forth, rocking me with her. "It's OK, everything will be OK," she whispered over and over. Her body was deeply familiar. I let myself be rocked and soothed, let the rocking of my body soothe her, but it was not OK—my mind fixed on its own dark mantra in counterpoint to hers.

Chapter Six

ALL THAT YEAR my mother would sit for hours in that high-backed armchair by the window in the living room, her legs tucked up under her. A well-worn paperback—on telepathy, or Edgar Cayce, or transcendental meditation—rested open on the arm of the chair. She studied the paranormal: reincarnation, Ouija boards, the lost island of Atlantis. She read Cayce again and again. I can imagine how she felt when the words of the books she read first sprang off the page, when they seemed to speak directly to her. For her it must have been that much more intense, more powerful than anything she'd known before, gaining speed and frequency until eventually she didn't need to read. The trail of words continued in her head. Then she spent her days chasing the flushed colors of her thoughts.

It was not a question of not seeing the forest for the trees—because she saw all that, the pine needles, the branches, the trunks, and the forest. Beyond that she saw the way the light flooded the forest canopy. And then the even deeper, untold meaning, the connection of the trees to the light and the branches to the needles. Everything was revealed. Unspeakable. Because the problem was. The problem was that the speed of thought was so much faster than the speed of words, the senses faster than thought, the speed of light faster still. And words hopelessly lumbering behind. There was sound. There was vision. There was light, and there were voices close by.

As she looked out across the cluttered room, everything she saw was alert with meaning—the royal blue of the carpets she had chosen, the orange of the bridge through the window, the fog just beginning to stream up the Bay—a world of color too bold, sound too sharp, every sensation overwrought. Sometimes beautiful, sometimes terrible. Was it easier for her when the fog rolled in for the afternoons, blanching the brilliant light?

She felt waves of power streaming from every object in that room: the clothes she wore, the food she ate, the things people gave her, the things she gave them. The objects around her created a current so complex, sometimes she could not navigate the room. Even if she wanted to go and stand at the window, she could not. She was locked in the tight embrace of the chair.

Garbage was a terrible vulnerability. The mail an unending burden. Bills, solicitations, junk mail, newspapers. They kept coming, and she could throw nothing away. The envelopes had her name, *Mrs. Russell B. Flynn*, printed in stark black ink across the front. She could not simply put them in the garbage and allow them to be taken away. To do so would open up a path that led straight back to her, a channel to her core. If matter could not be destroyed, how then could you ever extinguish the trails of influence that lingered on the things you touched? Forward and backward, we are linked in an unending chain, bound to everyone who's ever touched what we touch, to anyone who touches the things we touch after us. This is how evil circulates. This is how influence is exercised in the world.

Something fluttered at the edge of her vision. She turned her head sharply to the left. A hummingbird was feeding at the honeysuckle that grew beneath the window. She watched the emerald of his body, a steady form inside the rapid fluttering of his wings. She waited for them—now that the weather was warmer, they came everyday. Messengers. Lingering, suspended in the air, beating out a signal.

She'd been right to come here. The hummingbirds, the bridge. Proof. She knew she'd be girded here. This house, this room, this chair, the city, her fortress. She must operate from strength. She must cut her ties. The past was falling away, leaving a scaffold of stark connections. She had to make the connections. This bridge that came and went in and out of sight, blanketed by fog each day, had opened for its first test drive on May 10, 1937, the day she was born. Coincidence? No. They were bound. Daily she bore the weight of the cars across her spine. Daily they pressed against her, the good bearing her up, the bad wearing her down.

A battle was being waged, hidden from her before, hidden from other people still. The confirmation was in her dreams. On the television. In the newspapers. She'd always felt it, sensed a structure, a shape behind things. Now she knew. The world was in the thrall of a malevolent force. Proof. These battles on the street between young and old. Proof. Tear gas. Riots. Assassinations. Proof. And flame. The war. Babies, running naked in the burning light. Proof.

No one had any idea who she was. A laugh slipped through her lips as she thought of this. Cayce hadn't come this far. In the end he'd been weak. She was stronger. Stronger than he'd ever been. She'd come to the source. The very source. And they had spoken to her. They had told her who she was.

At first she'd resisted. She hadn't known who was speaking. She'd been terrified by their persistence, the shocking things they said. But now she could distinguish the higher voices, the ones that praised her, from the others, the bitter whisperers who laughed at her, at the paltry shape of her life. In the beginning she'd thought she would dissolve before all their noise and chatter. The constant harassment. Now she took the tight fizzle of their hissing whispers and drew them out, like a piece of gum stretched between her fingers. She pulled them so thin that they, not she, dissolved. This was her task. Her mission. Time. It took time. Darkness. And quiet. She needed the children to go to school. She needed the shades drawn against the sunlight. She needed the fog to cover the house.

Her eyes fixed on the hummingbird hovering below the window. She rocked in the chair. Her arms held her breasts tight against her chest. The motion brought her close to the source of her strength. She listened for the voices. Rocking, she entered the space before her. Rocking, space opened through the filtered light. Let it come, she thought. Let it come.

At this time, my father's friend Joe—now married and with two daughters of his own—lived in Santa Rosa, about an hour north of San Francisco. Joe was the only person my father confided in about my mother's condition. Every couple of weeks they'd meet at a bar halfway between Santa Rosa and the city. Joe has described these conversations to me: my father running through his options, which seemed to be narrowing, and all seemed to be bad, while Joe listened, nodding, waiting for my father to slowly circle towards the decision he had clearly already made in his bones.

I imagine them sitting in a booth, in a darkened corner of the bar, drinking Heinekens in the dark green bottle.

"Sally's crazy," my father says. He's said it so many times, in so many ways, it draws no response from Joe. Both of them know by now that in addition to all the things men generally mean when they say this about their wives—exasperation, incomprehension—it is also a statement of fact, the cold, hard, truth.

"I'm the focus of all her anger," my father says. "If I leave, maybe she'll calm down."

Joe nods.

My father returns to his hope that my mother's family, her brothers and her parents, who had all moved to Colorado a couple of years earlier, will be shaken into action if he leaves. That her parents, with whom she talks by phone every week, and who have so far tended to view my mother's troubles as marital, not mental, would intervene and succeed where he has failed. "Come out here. Make her get some help."

Not that he believes anymore—really believes—anyone can *make* her get help. She was a fixed and stubborn woman when they met. The more ill she becomes, the more unmovable she is. He's prodded, begged, and demanded that she see someone for the past two years. Nothing's moved her. Once, just once, he convinced her to let the minister from our church come over for a talk. The man sat on the living room couch facing my mother for fifteen minutes, mildly suggesting some marital counseling. My mother exploded, then hounded him out the door. After that we stopped going to church, cutting off the last outlet, the last group of people outside the family with whom she'd had contact.

My father came to a desperate two-part ultimatum: *Get some help, and clean up the house, or I'm leaving.* It was a full year later and she'd barely roused herself from the living room chair.

But still.

"I can't leave the girls," he says, shaking his head. "For god's sake, how can I leave them there?" he asks, as if Joe has any kind of answer to this.

Taking us with him is not a real option. My father explains to me now, "She was still so good with you guys. I couldn't imagine taking you away from her then."

But mostly he doesn't think of taking us because we are still more hers than his. She knows it, he knows it, and we know it.

And then there are the circular, sodden questions that have

to be asked until all hope is pounded out of them. "She's so smart, for Christ's sake," he says, "she's got to come out of this. Don't you think?"

Joe says the reasonable things. Time. Doctors. Hospitals. Medication.

"She's never taken a goddamn aspirin the whole time I've known her. Who the hell's going to get her to take medication?"

Before they leave, as he leans against the bar, waiting for change, my father turns to Joe and says, "She'll be OK for money. I'll always take care of that."

My own memories of this time are sketchy. The main things are that the apartment was always messy, my mother was always home, and my father was always angry. The mess didn't bother me. But when my father came home from work, the piles of newspapers, the games and toys we'd played with and abandoned throughout the day, the dishes from our snacks in the living room, many more dishes piled in the sink in the kitchen, suddenly looked bad. "Clean up this goddamn mess," he'd say, glowering at us from the couch while we scampered around, snatching up our dolls, gathering Monopoly money, stashing newspapers and magazines under the TV cart. It didn't help. The mess was implacable, and so was his anger.

Sometimes he came home wounded. He'd broken and sprained his ankles so many times playing sports in high school that once a group of medical students looking at his x-rays had decided that surely he couldn't walk. This didn't stop him from playing pickup basketball games at the playground down the block with guys ten and fifteen years younger than he was. These were tough games, fast and furious, no fouls called. Somebody always managed to come down on one of his ankles, neatly converting his psychic pain to physical injury.

He sat in the dining room with a pan of steaming water in front of him. I watched him from the living room. He pulled off his socks one at a time, wincing. Then slowly he peeled back the tight elastic braces he wore for sports. The skin underneath the braces did not match the rest of him. It was very white, and the dark hair that covered his legs didn't grow there. I stifled the urge to ask him if it hurt. I knew from experience that pain just made him another kind of mad. When he lowered his feet into the hot water, he made a noise that made me jump. The puffy skin around his ankle turned bright red. Then he put his feet in a pan of cold water and the skin went purple and blue.

Odd as it may seem, I don't remember being aware that anything was wrong with my mother. Perhaps that's because the one thing she kept up was being a mother. She still got my sisters and me off to school each day. Late, maybe, but off. Every day as I went out the back door, with the lunch she'd made me in my hand, she'd say, "Be a good girl at school today." As if I were ever anything but. When I got home, she was there in the living room, in her chair. Waiting, I thought. She still pored over my report cards and helped me with school projects. I took ballet lessons, and she came to the recitals. She drove Sara and me to the park every week for horseback riding lessons over the summer. She made dinner, and she still read to us from the Bible every night—still determined to get through the whole of it that year. Some stories she returned to again and again. There in the new apartment, the three of us circled around her on the floor in the living room, she read us the story of Jacob's Ladder. I don't remember exactly what she told us about this story, only that it mattered to her deeply. The images of Jacob climbing a ladder to the sky, and wrestling with an angel all night, have stayed with me to this day.

Each night she knelt with me and Amy by the side of our bunk beds in the room we shared. We recited the Lord's Prayer together. She kissed us and turned out the lights. She was never incoherent, and her anger, though scary, was aimed only at my father. She never yelled at us, not back then.

Still, when I put the school photos from first grade and second grade side by side, I can see a difference. In the first-grade photo I am a confident, smiling girl, dressed in a red jumper and white blouse, looking straight into the camera. In the second-grade photo, I'm not smiling. My mother doesn't seem to have made a special effort to dress me for picture day. My navy blue blouse is unbuttoned at the neck, hanging loosely against my pale skin. My head is tilted down and to the side. My eyes look overlarge, weighing down my whole face.

The fissure between my parents deepened. How could it not? They'd wrangled for years over the question of her getting help; the harder he pushed, the more she backed away, eyeing him with suspicion all the while.

As long as they'd been together they'd woken each morning and told each other their dreams. By now my mother used dreams, his and hers, to guide all decisions. My father says his dreams were by then so dark, so demon-haunted, he feared he would follow her right over the edge. That fear, more than anything, pushed him out the door. One morning he told her he wasn't going to talk about dreams anymore. He wasn't even going to think about them. And, he claims, he did not remember another dream for fifteen years.

Bad as this was for my father, my mother's terror must have been greater. She told me later she believed my father was the devil. No, that's not quite right. She didn't use the word *devil*. She said he was on the side of evil, more of a cohort, a higher-up in the devil's minions. How does that happen? How do you come to believe your husband of twelve years is in league with the devil?

Maybe it was one morning as she lay in bed watching him dress for work. Her eyes track him as he chooses a suit from the closet. He places the narrow tie around his neck. She examines the set of his jaw, the squint of his eyes, the shape of his hands as he knots the tie. Suddenly she jolts forward in terror. He turns to her, his face a tight mask, and behind that, nothing. It's all she can do to remain still while he bends and places a glancing kiss on her forehead. He turns and walks out of the room.

He's withholding his dreams. He goes to work in a rush of anger and comes home silent, bringing that hardness into the house. He watches the news. He yells at the children. His lust for the deals he makes at work hangs like a moldy film on his body. His voice is metallic and hard, distant, as if he's in the next room. Not right before her—telling her she needs help—she, who has struggled for his soul so long. She who has listened and interpreted for him, scouring both their dreams for signs. So many years, doing the work for both of them, for all of them. And now every gesture, every step confirms it: he's crossed the line.

And even then once she *knew*, was his old face restored to her from time to time? Were there still mornings when they talked, nights she turned to him and told him how frightened she was? Did their bodies still fit together in love?

The front door closes behind him. She sits up. Enveloped in terror, she rocks slowly on the edge of the bed. He's made a deal. He's crossed the line. He's on the other side. He'll take her down. He'll take the children down, if she lets him. She does the only thing possible: she steels herself against him, draws the children in tight, and prepares for battle.

My father remembers one last scene. He sat with my mother on a bench in Golden Gate Park in the late spring of 1974. My sisters and I were at school. He was home from work. In fact, he hadn't worked much that year, hadn't closed a deal, hadn't earned a dime in months.

"Sally," he said, "I can tell you exactly what's going to happen." She didn't look at him. "First, you're going to lose me," he said. "Then I'm going to take the children." She turned slightly, her gaze flickered over him. "You'll lose the house," he went on. "You'll end up living in one of my buildings in the Tenderloin."

She shook her head. She almost laughed. She didn't argue.

Everything he said was beside the point. Her mind was fixed on something else altogether. Then turning full on him, her eyes focusing in for just a second, she said sharply, "No one will ever give *you* the children."

On the day my father finally moved out, after he'd shuttled his suitcases to the car and the front door closed behind him, my mother turned to us and said, "There goes a very bad man." Her words startled me, but I didn't doubt her. Doubting her was not yet a part of my makeup. And now that she said it, now that she put it that way, it seemed true. He hadn't been very nice for a long time, and he was leaving us—that was bad.

My mother sat up tall in her high-backed gold armchair and spoke almost without malice. She was calm—surprisingly so under the circumstances. My sisters and I sat across from her, lined up on the living room couch. It was the first day of summer between second and third grade. I don't remember the days that led up to this one, if there had been more fights—surely there were—or if I'd known ahead of time he was leaving. Just this scene: my father carrying suitcases out to his car, my sisters and I very quiet on the couch. He came back to kiss each of us on the forehead before he left. I didn't look him in the eye. My mother's coiled anger trumped whatever sympathy I had for him—trumped everything, in fact.

When the door closed, I turned to look out the window behind me and caught the back of my father's head, craning slightly forward as he walked down the staircase to the street.

He wore a corduroy jacket, lemon-colored, with patches at the elbows. For a second I saw the spot at the top of his head where, at thirty-four, his scalp was just beginning to show through.

"A very bad man," she repeated with a rapid movement of her head that shook the dark, loose curls of her hair. "This summer we will erase the past," my mother said after he drove away. She held up her arm, an imaginary eraser in her hand, and swept the air in front of her. "We'll wipe the slate clean."

We sat there for a long time that day. My mother laid out the new terms of our lives. They had to do with staying inside and cutting all our ties to other people, with being careful about what we ate and what we wore.

Across town, in the one-bedroom apartment he'd rented the week before, my father—whom I've never seen shed more than a few tears—cried for two days.

From my perch on the living room couch, I watched the fog flow in like a second body of water over the Bay. When it was rolling in I could see where it ended, where it began. I could watch its shape change as it came slowly towards us. First the bridge disappeared, then the trees in the Presidio, then the houses and the street down below. And then suddenly, there was nothing to see. The fog was just a white melancholy that hung in the air, punctuated by the double wail of the foghorns, low, and lower, moaning through the afternoon. Gazing into the distanceless space, there was no way to know the whole world wasn't like this: muffled and dim, shrouded in white.

PART TWO *Drowning*

Chapter Seven

AFTER MY FATHER LEFT the shades went down, and the acacia tree in the front yard grew up over the windows. My mother didn't leave the house for months at a time, and for three full years no one came inside. Days slid into night and night into day. Bedtime receded; mealtimes dissolved. The house grew messier and messier. My mother more and more manic, hovering over our every move, then by turns impassive, retreating to her room or to the enlarged universe inside her head.

My memory of those three years remains cordoned off from the rest of my life. The images are sharp, but there's a sequencing problem, a tendency for scenes to repeat. When I try to bring order, I get no traction. My memory is compressed, as if everything that happened inside that house during the whole of those three years is singular—one long unrelieved bad dream.

I want to say *fog*. I want to say *shade*. I want to say the air was thick, movement ponderous, as if we were underwater. I want to say it was an effort to raise our limbs, that we all heard voices whispering in the hall, but of course none of that is true. My mother heard voices; we heard only her whispered responses, the crackling laughter that slipped through her lips, the muffled sobs from behind her bedroom door, the pulse of her anger rising around us.

Outside the house, my life moved along at an even pace. Weekends with my father, vacations to the beach. Hot days in September, cooler days of fall. Third grade: Mrs. Pirelli; fourth grade: Mr. Stover; fifth grade: Mrs. Collins. Field trips to the Mint, ferry rides to Angel Island. Cursive, fractions, kickball, dodgeball, being chased by the boys at recess. Lisa Adelson and Laurie Mori, and Fiona, whose last name I cannot recall, whom we called fleabag and kept at the margin of our circle because she was a Jehovah's Witness and couldn't say the Pledge of Allegiance or go to birthday parties. Seagulls pick at our lunch leavings on the pavement of the schoolyard. And on rainy days we cram three to a seat, wet plastic slicker against wet plastic slicker, into the school bus. I watch the lightning through rain-battered windows, then splash through puddles arm-in-arm with Lisa, my best friend, whose house in the long afternoons after school will become a refuge.

But inside our house, time refused to flow in a normal way, as if the density of my mother's illness pulled at its very fabric.

What grew, the progression I hold onto even now, was my own awareness of her illness. That first summer after my father left, it was just presentiment, an unformed sense of dread. I still saw the world through the glass of her perception. The distortions in the lens troubled me, but I had no language for what was wrong.

Stuck inside the house with my mother, who was intent on unwriting our lives, erasing the past, and cutting all our ties, my sisters and I grasped for a narrative that would hold. We spent our days playing dolls, telling each other stories of loss, abandonment, and escape over and over again. Every game began like this: "We're orphans," I'd say, or Sara would say. Then we'd dispense with parents by way of illness, train wreck, or civil war.

Only Amy didn't want to be an orphan. But then she was lucky to be playing with us at all. Up until then, Sara and I had only let her watch while we primped our dolls for fancy dress balls, then swirled them with imaginary partners on the parquet floor in the dining room. Now that we had let her in, the game had changed.

The three of us were gathered in the room Amy and I shared, all still in our nightgowns—there were more than a few days that summer when we did not get dressed. We rarely left the house. My mother did not leave at all. Our Little Women dolls—sent to us by my grandma Sadie for Christmas—were spread on the floor in front of us, their long dresses fanning over their legs. These dolls, with their Victorian-era clothing, petticoats, aprons, stockings, and long hair that could be brushed and styled, had displaced all the rag dolls and stuffed animals that made up our menagerie before. I'd abandoned Big Baby for good, and an era in which all our games took place in "olden days" had begun.

Meg was Sara's doll, Amy was Amy's, and Jo was mine.

Beth—who was technically my mother's—was a hot potato. Doomed, in her pale pink dress.

"You can be Beth if you want," I said to Amy.

"I don't wanna be Beth," Amy answered. "You guys are gonna make her die."

"No," I said, glancing at Sara. "We won't." She could go blind, I thought. She could be crippled.

Amy looked to Sara.

"We promise," Sara said.

The six years between them gave Sara room to mother Amy. She was right on my heels; I didn't cut her any slack.

Amy and I were wearing pink and white nylon shifts, faded from much washing. Matching, because my mother always bought two of something she liked, which was fine in the beginning when the clothes were new and I wore the small dress and Sara the bigger one. By the time the larger dress was tight on me, and my mother still insisted that Amy and I wear them, the whole matching business lost its charm.

Sara's nightgown barely covered her knees when she stood up. The three of us had always been evenly spaced in height: Sara was just able to rest her chin comfortably on the top of my head, and I could do the same to Amy. But this summer, Sara had shot up. I was only to her shoulder now. The baby fat on my limbs and belly matched Amy, not Sara. Worse, Sara was growing breasts under there. Already it was getting harder to lure her into our games. She thought she was too old to play dolls with us. I had to make the game particularly intriguing to keep her.

"The lady at the orphanage is very mean. We have to run away and go west," I said. Sara and I were in thrall to the prairie. We were racing each other through the *Little House on the Prairie* books. A trip to the bookstore on Clement Street was one of the few outings my mother would still sanction.

I seized on the idea of getting real provisions for the journey west and interrupted the game to run to the kitchen. In the hall I heard the radio, Charley Pride singing "Kiss an Angel Good Morning," and behind that the hum of the sewing machine. I found myself singing along. *And love her like the devil when you get back home.* My mother kept the radio on and tuned to the country music station pretty much all the time.

Dishes from last night's dinner were piled around the sink in the kitchen. Boxes of Wheat Chex and Special K, milk cartons, finished but not thrown away, cluttered the counters. The garbage can overflowed. In the corner tiny flies hovered over the fruit bowl. A piece of bread, toasted but forgotten, waited in the hollow of the smooth silver toaster.

I got a chair and pulled the boxes down off the shelf. Flour, sugar, and salt don't rot. I poured out rations in plastic bags and took them back to our bedroom.

We picked out the two strongest-looking specimens from Sara's model horse collection. We bundled up all the extra doll clothes, piled in the sacks of salt and sugar, then packed the Little Women in. They stood up ramrod straight in the back of Amy's circus wagon.

Sara walked the horses forward. I pushed the wagon. Amy scooted along on her knees in front of us, clearing a path in the hallway. Without my father, there was nothing to impede the messiness of the house. My sisters and I didn't clean. My mother had always done the housework. We knew she didn't want things disturbed. The rules were complicated and ever changing, but *don't throw anything away* stayed firm.

We decided to make camp on the shore of the Mississippi River. We had to cross before spring—before the ice broke. The game stalled there because Sara and I could not agree on which state the Mississippi was in. I was a stickler for authenticity and historical detail, so I went to the dining room to ask my mother.

My mother sat at the end of the dining room table, her head bent over the sewing machine. She wore a white terrycloth bathrobe with a zipper up the front. She'd grown larger during the past year. Her hair curled in around her neck, but not stylishly as it once had; now it was just overgrown. The first gray hairs clustered at her part. I don't know what happened to the round John Lennon glasses—or the sensibility that chose them—but now she wore glasses with gray plastic rims, the kind that swoop down, telescoping not only her eyes but the skin under her eyes, which had grown coarse and bagged. She'd stopped taking care of herself, but it was more than that. Those few years wrought rapid changes on my mother's body. Almost overnight she transformed from a striking young woman to the shapeless, ageless person she would remain for the next twenty-five years.

The room was dim, the shades were drawn, but the little light on the sewing machine illuminated a circle of fabric directly in front of her. My mother's foot moved steadily up and down on the pedal of the sewing machine. The needle raced, then slowed as she let up on the pedal. She placed her right hand on the wheel to lift the needle, shifted the fabric, brought the needle down again, pressed the pedal, and then set the needle trotting back over the same seam.

The table was covered with her sewing materials: piles of fabric, some with thin patterns pinned to them, bobbins, thimbles, plastic cases of sewing needles, a plump cushion sprouting straight pins, packets of buttons and snaps still on the cardboard, and rolls of fat white elastic that come wound like shoelaces, which my mother sewed into the waists of the pants she made for us.

She had a large clear plastic box for storing spools of thread. When I was younger I loved to play with the thread, rearranging the spools to make new patterns with the colors, putting them in the order of the rainbow. I'd go through the little compartments and examine the buttons my mother collected: tortoiseshell, bone, metal, gold, brass, and silver. Now the box yawned open on the table. Half the spools of thread were missing from their pegs, buried under the fabric, or fallen under the table, where they would in time unwind and tangle with stray scraps of elastic, or the black cords of zigzag edging my mother sometimes sewed on blouses. Already the thick black basting thread was twined with the yellow measuring tape and lacing its way across the long formal table where we used to eat.

"It depends," my mother said, in answer to my question about the Mississippi. She got up heavily from the chair and

dug the *New York Times Atlas* out of a pile of books on the floor
in the corner of the dining room. She showed me the fat blue
line of the Mississippi River running clear down the middle of
the country. She pointed out the town on the banks of the Mississippi in southern Illinois where she was born. I decided that
was where we would cross.

I passed back through the living room, joining Loretta Lynn
briefly for the second verse of "Coal Miner's Daughter." Since
my father had left, we'd had this strange new music—Conway
Twitty, Dolly Parton, and Glen Campbell—on all the time. For-
eign, twangy, alien, mournful, this music was from some part
of the country, some way of life I was not familiar with. The
singers rolled out their words in a deep, slow complaint, drawing out the vowels as if each one had to be carried up from the
coalmine by hand. It was not a happy music. But the lyrics were
great, the songs told stories, and it was easy to sing along. You
could usually guess what was coming—these singers went for
the rhyme, no matter how far the stretch. Only my tongue tangled trying to get "hard" to rhyme with "tired."

Since my mother had determined not to leave the house
at all that summer, Sara and I did the grocery shopping. Every
few days we made a trip to a mom-and-pop store five blocks
from our house, bringing home all we could carry in a single
trip. Sara was eleven. I was seven. My mother would write out
a list for us on adding machine paper while we got dressed to
go outside, pulling on our homemade duds, polyester tops,
and elastic-waist pants, searching out our tennis shoes from

the piles in the living room or bedrooms. If we couldn't get a brush through our hair, we'd tie a bandana over it.

In the store Sara would hold the scrolling list in her hand and send me out for two or three items at a time. We'd meet back at the cart to consult the list again. Inevitably, there were things we couldn't find. Then we'd whisper together in the aisle, weighing whether to ask for help. The owner, the butcher, and the checkout guys all knew us. They knew my mother too, from before when she'd shopped with one or another of us in tow. They were unfailingly nice to us. We found this mortifying.

Asking for help was dicey because, though the grocer could easily find the items on the list, he did not appreciate the importance of getting the brand my mother asked for. Hunt's tomato paste was good; Del Monte no good, in a way we could not explain. We found everything on our own and tried to get in and out of the store before anyone could ask if we needed help.

The vegetable freezer we faced together. The long metal bin with sliding glass doors on top wasn't always well stocked, which meant the boxes of frozen spinach, broccoli, and fancy mixed vegetables that my mother wanted were all the way down at the bottom. Neither Sara nor I could reach in that far. We waited until no one was in the aisle, then I plunged in, head first, feet dangling off the floor, the metal side of the freezer slicing me in two at the waist. Sara held on to the elastic at the back of my pants so I wouldn't fall in.

At the checkout counter, we watched warily as the grocer rang up each item. My eyes tracked between his hands and the register. When the total came up, Sara pulled out the wadded bills my mother had given her. We were short. Again.

I looked at Sara and then at the pile of food before us, trying to figure out what we could safely put back. But it was her call: she had the list; she had the money. She lifted a pound of spaghetti, set it back down, lifted the dishwasher detergent, hesitated. "Is this enough?" she asked, picking up a can of tuna (Chicken-of-the-Sea, never, never, Bumble Bee).

The grocer took the tuna from Sara. Pushing the can back across the counter, he said, "That's OK. Just tell your mother you owe me two dollars and forty-five cents. Next time."

I cast a nervous glance at Sara. This seemed worse. Owing.

The grocer took his time bagging. He distributed everything carefully, separating the half-gallon milk cartons, lifting each bag to test the weight. When he was done there were three bags for Sara, two for me.

He handed me my two bags slowly. "That OK?" he asked. How must we have appeared to him? Shy, long-faced girls, unusually close, and close-mouthed. I mumbled, "It's OK," from behind the paper, anxious to wiggle loose from his gaze.

We walked the five blocks home as fast as we could. The serrated tops of the bags cut into my chin as they bobbed up with each step. My fingers got numb from clutching the coarse brown paper, so we had to stop every half block and rest on someone's stoop. Then we'd shift the bags between us and set off again.

Getting home, getting the key in the door and the door closed tight behind us—quickly, so that if anyone was in the hall, they couldn't see into our apartment—was a relief. We were friendly with all the neighbors. Mrs. Franks, the elderly lady who lived upstairs, sometimes invited Sara and Amy and me for tea. But it was awkward to see them now since no one was allowed in our apartment anymore. The weight of the bags was nothing compared to the pressure of people's eyes upon me. Outside, I could not help knowing that our lives were strange and wrong. The messy house, Sara and I doing the grocery shopping—and not just going for a quart of milk, but all of it—staying inside all the time, weird country music that the neighbors complained about. And my mother. She was not like anyone else. I knew it, though I could not have explained exactly how. Just that she was shameful and that hiding our lives from the world required constant vigilance. Sara must have felt it even more acutely than I did. She was coming up fast on adolescence, straining at the bit, but in my eagerness to keep up, I took in the censure of the world early.

Once inside the house, I went straight to the big chair in front of the window in the living room and sank into my book. The part of that summer that I didn't spend playing dolls with my sisters, I spent slumped in that chair: head against one armrest, one leg flopped over the other, inhaling the classics of children's literature, gathering up plotlines for our games.

I read with the intensity of a novice. The boundaries between books and life were not yet fixed. I entered wholly into whatever lush and lovely world was available: *Charlotte's Web, Black Beauty, Heidi, Little Women*—books not only lovely, but full of heartbreak. From early on, crying and reading went together.

I remember a long afternoon curled in my chair reading the last third of *Little Women*, after Beth died, through tears. Those losses felt as real to me as any loss I had ever suffered. Or maybe they were just cleaner.

Mostly that summer I read the *Little House on the Prairie* books. Sara and I bought them in pairs and then drew straws— toothpicks my mother broke in half and hid in her fist—over who got to read the books in the right order. On the cover of my book, a barefoot girl ran through high grass. On Sara's book, a girl on horseback in a bright red dress rode without a saddle, her body flat and low, straining forward, across the back of the galloping stallion. *The Little House on the Prairie* books weren't steeped in tragedy like the other books I was drawn to, but they had a deep hold on me. The main character, the writer herself, was the middle of three girls, named Laura, and she, like me, had brown hair. *Little House in the Big Woods* was the first "chapter" book I read. When I finished it, I told both my parents, and anyone else who asked, that I was going to be a writer when I grew up. To prove it, I started writing little stories in notebooks.

The doll game went on for weeks. The ice broke while we were crossing the Mississippi; we barely managed to forge the rest of the way across. We built a dugout house on the prairie, planted crops, lost them to locusts, survived a barren winter, went further west. It took most of the summer to get our wagon train out to California. In the living room, we staked our claim before the bay windows, in sight of the Pacific. We cleared space at the foot of the green couches. With a ruler Sara marked the borders of our homestead. She made nice, even hatches in the carpet, which looked the way farmland looks from an airplane. I got the Lincoln logs and we built a cabin. The scale was all off—the dolls could never have fit in a Lincoln log house—but the cabin looked right next to the patchwork fields, sturdy enough to weather a storm.

Chapter Eight

ON FRIDAY AFTERNOONS my father came to get us for the weekends. I'd watch for his cream-colored Mercedes from the window in the living room. Sometimes he came later than he'd promised, and I'd pass the time counting cars. *Daddy's will be the tenth car to come down the street.* When the tenth car passed and he still hadn't come, I'd try a bigger number. Or I'd try to guess, to practice my ESP by closing my eyes and letting the number come to me.

Usually it was when I gave up waiting, when I picked up a book or wandered back to my bedroom to do homework, that he came. The three of us ran down to the street with backpacks full of clothes for the weekend. He never came up, which was fine. Keeping things calm between my parents meant keeping them apart.

In the car, as we headed to the still unfamiliar part of the city where he lived, my father would ask about our week. He'd want to know if we'd played outside, if we'd gotten out of the house. Since he was clearly much happier if we said we'd been outside, we were in the habit of saying yes, even when we hadn't.

"How's your mother?" he'd ask, drawing out the final two words as if putting "your" and "mother" together had become hard work—emphasis on the possessive pronoun. He'd always called her this: your mother. But his removal from the scene changed the meaning of the term. What bound my parents together could be dissolved. She was rapidly unbecoming his wife. But she was ours forever. Immutably. Even more so now. Whatever dread and strain weighed upon his words accrued automatically to us.

"Fine," I'd answer. Or Sara would answer. And Amy kept quiet, because she knew the drill, knew we didn't want her to talk. Though we never discussed it among ourselves, we knew our parents were at war, knew we were the territory under dispute, and knew that the less information we gave to either party, the smoother things would be for us. We were unified, bound by the first commandment of sibling loyalty—the coerced, whispered, or hissed imprecation—*don't tell*.

My father's new apartment was spotless, with glossy hardwood floors and a sparkling kitchen, or so it seemed to me. Now I realize it was just a one-bedroom in an older high-rise building. My sisters and I slept in rainbow-striped sleeping bags, two on the living room floor, one on the couch. In the morning, my father made pancakes and bacon on the tiny grill in his kitchen. Dinner we ate out.

During the day he took us swimming, at public pools or at the home of friends of his who lived in Marin County (who had their own swimming pool!). We went to the park, to the beach, to Angel Island on the ferry. Overnight he became like a dad on TV again: telling us funny stories while we hiked up Mount Tam, giving shoulder rides to Amy when she was tired, playing shark in the pool and overturning our rafts, coaxing me from the end of the diving board.

I remember a poolside afternoon that summer. The four of us were assembling salami sandwiches in someone else's kitchen. I was barefoot on the cool tile, a heavy towel wrapped round my waist over my swimsuit, wet hair clumped across my forehead, chlorine biting in my eyes. My father handed me a soda. He noted that he saw us more now that we spent weekends with him than he did before he moved out. I smiled up at him, teeth against the edge of the glass, the carbonated mist of 7-Up (forbidden by my mother) tickling my nose: "You're nicer now than you were then too." He laughed, loose enough now to be teased.

On a rainy day, when finally it just wasn't possible to go outside, we bought a new Monopoly set for my father's apartment. We'd been playing Monopoly since we were old enough to roll dice. Our games were long, intense, and hard fought. My father had his own rules, which changed over time, growing more complex as we got older.

I had to have the railroads, all four of them. I liked the steady income—two hundred dollars a pop each time someone landed on one, something I could count on even if they never gained value, could never be improved. No amount of steady losses could convince me that trading valuable property to get those railroads was not a winning strategy.

My father had no sentimental favorites when it came to property. He employed a high-risk, opportunistic strategy, buying every property he landed on and going into debt early in the game to do it. His rules allowed for bank loans and mortgages on properties you already owned, creative financing to make new purchases. He engineered complex swaps, three-way trades if need be, to put together monopolies. Then he started making improvements, putting houses on all his properties to crank up the rents. His rules encouraged more wheeling and dealing than the rules on the box top did, making it possible for a single player to accumulate great wealth.

He cupped his hands together, brought the dice to his mouth to blow on, shook them, caught my eye in exaggerated glee, tossed them with a flourish, and said, "OK, you turkeys, read 'em and weep."

He pounded his marker—the cowboy boot, he was always the cowboy boot—around the board. Inevitably his marker came down just where he wanted it to—on Kentucky Avenue, say, when he already had Illinois and Indiana. He grinned, looked up at us, then stuck out his tongue, curling it so it flared at the sides, then came to a fine point, which he planted firmly, intently on the end of his long nose: tip of tongue to tip of nose, his quintessential gesture, accompanied by a self-appreciative laugh, an exclamation point on acts of skill, luck, and cunning. When he landed a shot in the garbage can, or found a parking spot right in front of the restaurant, he did this sly little victory dance, which echoed the crude *nyah nyah nyah* tongue sticking of childhood, but had been refined over the years into this more dexterous, self-referential, elegant, if you will, flourish. The tongue, turned back on itself, pointed not to the defeat of the opponent but rather to the prowess of the victor.

My sisters and I practiced long and hard to capture this gesture. It was beyond our reach. Lacking sufficient length of nose or tongue to pull it off with ease, we had to strain and pull. And if you have to strain, well, the effect is lost. The best we could hope for was to be on the inside of his gesture—to share his glee. He always won. That was a given. For us, the trick was how to maneuver to make sure we were on his team or, failing that, how to enjoy the reflected glow of his glory.

A few hours later, my father had monopolies covering half the board and four houses on every property. My sisters and I held our breath when we rolled. Sara and I had a couple of monopolies each, but we couldn't buy houses because there weren't any left. And my father would never convert to hotels and free up the houses when he had us over a barrel like this. Amy was always the first to succumb; she didn't put up much of a fight. When she landed on one of his properties and couldn't pay, she handed over everything she had to him and became his "limited partner." For the rest of the game he'd whisper strategy in her ear, and her eyes beamed as she nodded along.

Sara and I had to soldier on. He always had some scheme to bail us out and keep us in the game. He'd take the railroads off my hands when I owed him money, in a kind of pawn arrangement where he'd get the two hundred bucks every time someone landed on a railroad until I could get them out of hock. He gave good, honest advice. But mostly he taught by example. Think big, take risks, show mercy only when you've already got your opponent pinned down. The rest of the game was a slow bleed; the only real contest was to see who could last longer, Sara or me. In the end my father got title to everything.

We didn't mind; we felt lucky to be playing with him at all.

When Sunday afternoon came, we all turned glum, my father included. We were quiet in the car. As he dropped us off, my father would hand Sara the check for alimony and child support. The three of us made the slow walk up the long concrete stairs to the sidewalk above the street—then on up into our building. We could feel my mother watching from the window.

She did not actively obstruct our seeing my father, but she wanted us to spend as little time in his presence as possible. The time of our return was one of the fronts in the multipronged battle she waged against my father. My father, feeling we needed as much sunlight, oxygen, and freedom as he could supply, tried to stretch thirty-six hours into forty-eight.

The radio greeted us when we came in the door. Something mournful and sad like "Rhinestone Cowboy." My mother gave each of us a hug and a kiss, pulling us back into her hawkish possession. Then she sat us down in the living room to give a full report on the weekend, beginning with what we ate on Friday night.

"Hamburgers," Sara said.

"Did he make them, or did you go out?" she asked.

My mother didn't see my father face-to-face very often, but he loomed large in her imagination. She tried to gauge the extent of his influence over us. Every detail counted. I'd gotten in the habit of rehearsing what I'd tell her in my head on the car ride home. Coming up the stairs, I'd search for innocuous phrases. A neutral tone. Not as if we enjoyed being with my father, but not showing any sign of distress either.

"We went out," I said.

"Where?"

"To Clown Alley," I said.

"Which one?"

"The one on Columbus," Sara said.

"Then what?"

"Then nothing. We went to bed," Sara said.

"Did you see anyone else?"

"No," we answered in unison.

"Did you take a shower?"

Sara and I both hesitated, careful not to look at each other. My mother didn't want us to take showers at my father's house. Something to do with washing off the protective halo of her influence, which we carried on our bodies when she bathed us, the same aura that clung to the clothes she made for us by hand. But you couldn't really explain all that to my father or refuse to bathe at his house.

"No," I lied.

My mother rubbed her hands as she listened to us. Her skin was shiny and distressed. She had ailments, itchy rashes that crawled up her fingers. Her toes were afflicted as well. The nail on her little toe grew straight up—thick and yellow.

I watched her face, her movements. I gauged my story by the tone of her voice, the rise and fall of her interest, shifting topics when she got too interested, going on and on when her attention drifted, trying to sound as if I were withholding nothing, but not being expansive either, because then her grilling would never end. A space opened between my thoughts and my words. It yawned wider over the years. The habit of rehearsing everything I said would become so ingrained, I no longer even noticed.

I glanced into the dining room. A piece of cardboard covered the lower half of one of the windows. I stared for a moment and then looked quickly away so my mother would not notice me looking at it. I didn't dare ask her what had happened.

"Daddy told us a story about a book he read," I said.

"What book?"

"About Russia," said Sara. My father often worked from books or movies when he told stories. This particular weekend he'd told two, one based on a history of the Russian Revolution he was reading and one based on the plot of the movie *Deliverance*. Don't ask me why.

"What was the story?" my mother asked.

"About the czar," I said, hoping to steer clear of *Deliverance*. She nodded for me to go on.

"And his family," I said, stopping short. This was bad too. I didn't want to tell her about the czar's family getting shot. So, scrambling, I told her it was about Rasputin instead.

"Rasputin?"

Too late I realized the dead czarinas were nothing compared to the demonic otherworldliness of Rasputin. She made us tell her the whole story over again. Three times.

"I don't remember anything else," I said. "Just he cured the czar's son from bleeding to death, that's all."

"But you said he had long fingernails?"

"Yeah."

"What did your father say about that?"

I shrugged.

Sara shrugged.

Finally we took showers—Sara in the bathroom off her bedroom, Amy and I in the bathroom we shared with my mother. She stood next to me by the tub, while the water poured over me. Though I was nearly eight, my mother always washed my hair and Amy's hair herself. She was tense, her knuckles rough against my scalp as she scrubbed, presumably rinsing me clean of my father's influence.

Afterwards, the three of us sat on the living room floor, watching the *Wonderful World of Disney* with towels turbaned around our wet hair. My mother made Sloppy Joes for dinner—she was back on meat now. We ate in front of the TV. She sat in her chair behind us, knees tucked under her.

"Why did your father tell you this story?" she asked.

I turned around to look at her. "He likes to tell us history." I turned back to the TV, but I knew she would not let it rest. She would return to this story again and again over the next week.

All that summer we shuttled between parents, learning how to navigate the terrain between them. By learning what to say to each of them, I managed to be loyal to both. I could even think one thing with my father, another with my mother. My father regained our favor almost effortlessly with pancakes and hikes, the orderliness of his home, and the irresistible draw of his charm. In my heart I no longer believed he was "a bad man." He was a winner, and if you were on his team, you'd always win too. But even knowing that, if I'd had to choose between them right there, right then, I'd still have chosen her—down with the ship if it came to that. She commanded my loyalty and love in a way my father never could, partly because he didn't demand it. He didn't mind if we loved her too, and anyway he could get along without us. He'd land on his feet no matter what. With my mother there was no guarantee. You were either with her or against her, and in that demand for absolute loyalty lay an unspeakable need. She was our mother; the whole of her will was bent on holding us to her. If one of us betrayed her, what would happen? And without us, what would she be?

In August 1974, two things happened that remain connected in my mind. My mother got divorce papers from my father in the mail, and the president resigned. My mother was very happy about the resignation, but not about the divorce papers. Not because she objected to the divorce, but because she'd planned to file first. She just hadn't gotten around to it. Getting the papers in the mail made her furious. It proved just how sneaky my father was: planning all the time, strategizing against her, getting the jump.

We sat on the living room floor and watched the president on TV. His cheeks trembled as he spoke. My sisters and I cheered. The hatred we felt for him was very pure. He was a bad guy—both my parents agreed.

"The tide is turning," my mother said quietly, from her chair. I turned my head to look back at her. She meant more than the White House.

She could name the forces of evil. Rasputin, Nixon, Kissinger, Lee Harvey Oswald, Del Monte, Mattel, Lieutenant William Calley: they were all on the list, forces whose influence extended back and forth through time. Playing with a toy made by Mattel, taking a bite of food made by Del Monte, hearing a story about Rasputin—these things marked you as indelibly as napalm. She didn't say it directly, but I knew my father was on that list too.

I listened to her. Took in every word she said. I carved out a place for them in my mind. Doubt and belief were beside the point. I lived in her world, was latched to her side; I needed to understand the rules.

My mother's family—my grandparents, aunts, uncles, and fifteen cousins—lived in Colorado at this time, and each summer the whole clan gathered for a reunion at a church camp in the Rocky Mountains. We hadn't been for two years, though my mother kept promising us a trip. She was still in close touch with her parents. And there had been phone calls back and forth all summer, Amos and Sadie urging my mother to come for the reunion, my mother equivocating. We packed our suitcases—they sat in the front hall for two weeks, but our departure date kept slipping. My mother even bought plane tickets. Only we never made it to the airport.

After he moved out, my father phoned my mother's parents and begged them to get more involved, to come out and see my mother, to intervene where he had failed. My grandparents were in a tough spot. My father was the estranged husband, and my mother their favored child. Why should they listen to him? Plus they had no daily contact with my mother, and she could be quite convincingly sane, particularly on the phone. Not to mention a little intimidating. And most of all, it was just too painful for them to believe she was ill, even though they'd been through this before.

Amos's older brother Frank had had similar trouble. It started one morning in the mid-1940s when Frank's wife called Amos for help. He found Frank locked in a bedroom, exhausted after a long night up "fighting the devil." Frank had an iron poker from the stoker furnace in his hand. He'd somehow bent it into a perfect circle. Did my mother know about this? Or about the little book Frank wrote that described a hitherto unknown force that repelled just as surely as gravity pulled? Did she know about Frank's hospitalizations, about the electric shock and insulin shock therapy he received over the years? I know only because late in life Amos recounted this story in the autobiography he wrote for his grandchildren. Did my mother know, did any of them know, that there is a genetic component to mental illness?

We never made it to Colorado that summer. In fact, my mother never got on an airplane again. She must have felt she owed us a trip, though. The week before school began she roused herself, left the house for the first time in months, and took the three of us on an impromptu midweek car trip.

We drove up to Clear Lake, a sleepy resort town northeast of San Francisco. We listened to country music on the radio, singing along with the now familiar voices of Merle Haggard, Mel Tillis, and Tammy Wynette, whose D-I-V-O-R-C-E song seemed to play every hour. It felt vaguely dangerous to have my mother at the wheel—my father had always driven on all our trips.

The hotel where we stayed had a miniature golf course. I could not have been more charmed: moving drawbridges, tiny castles, waterfalls, little German towns. My mother was surprisingly good. After three days at the hotel, Sara and I were gaining on her, just a few points off par.

I felt certain my father would be happy to hear about our trip. We had been out of the house for three days. Plus, miniature golf was a sport. He'd like that. When we piled into the car the next Friday and told him about the trip, he didn't say anything. He let us chatter on as we drove to Vince's, the neighborhood Italian restaurant we'd been going to for years, even back when we lived on 12th Avenue. People crowded into the front vestibule, lined up waiting for tables. Toni, our waitress, gave my father the high sign, and we slipped past the line, into a booth in Toni's territory, where an open Heineken was already waiting for my father on the table.

My father fished change for the jukebox from his pocket— three songs for a dime. Each booth had its own machine. Plastic grape leaves hung from the ceiling. The oil paintings on the walls were of ships in the harbor of Genoa, the city Toni and Vince, the owner, had left twenty years before. I flipped through the metal pages inside the glass bubble on the wall. I chose "Blue Suede Shoes," Sara picked "Fifty Ways to Leave Your Lover," and Amy chose "Tie a Yellow Ribbon 'Round the Old Oak Tree." The sap.

Toni came back with three glasses cupped together between her hands. The milk came in small thin glasses, and it was always just slightly warm.

"A cannelloni, and three half and halfs?" she said, writing the order on her pad before we even nodded back at her. Half and half—half spaghetti, half ravioli.

There'd been a rough spot at the start of summer when we'd started coming without my mother, and my father had had to explain to Toni and Vince that they'd separated, but now everything was running smoothly.

Amy asked if she could go up front and watch Vince toss

the pizzas. My father nodded, and she slid out of the booth, a month shy of her fifth birthday but already at ease in the crowd. She made her way to the front of the restaurant and stood beside the stainless steel counter to charm and be charmed by Vince, his eyes moving easily between her and the white dough, which he first punched, then tossed on his fists higher and higher into the air.

After she left, my father turned to us.

"If your mother took you away some place, like Portland, you'd call me, wouldn't you?" he asked.

"Why would Mommy take us to Portland?" I asked.

"Say she did."

"We've never been to Portland," I said.

"We'd call," Sara said.

He looked at me. I nodded. "We'd call," I said, sipping my milk, trying to make it last until the half and half came.

He made Sara and me repeat his telephone number out loud three times each.

Chapter Nine

THE BELL SOUNDED, and thirty-five pairs of eyes turned to Mrs. Pirelli, who stood at the front of my third-grade classroom. "Earthquake drill," she said, and then, with a downward motion of her hands, "Drop." We dove under our desks, doing the California version of duck and cover, turning our backs on the windows to shield our heads from falling glass. There wasn't enough desk cover for all of us. We giggled and squirmed, banging our heads up against the metal undersides of the desks, but we were not afraid. It was just a drill. And in any case, earthquakes didn't scare us. They came with the territory.

Personally I liked earthquakes, even hoped for them. When I woke in the night and the windows were rattling or the bed was softly shifting under me, I felt more excited than afraid. In the morning I'd go to my mother's room and get in bed with her for a few minutes before getting ready for school. She'd ask if I'd felt the quake, and I'd remember it like a dream. We'd listen to the news on her clock radio to find out how big it had been. I rooted for high scores, and though I have no solid evidence for this, I have the feeling my mother did too.

The biggest quake I'd ever been through was in the fives, which rattled the house but did not break anything. I wanted to know what a six felt like. My mother had explained, my teachers had explained, about the Richter scale. How it is exponential, how eight is much, much bigger than two times four. But still.

Ritchie Meyers crawled over from another desk to get next to me. I stopped giggling and scrambled over Lisa, my best friend, to make sure he didn't touch me. He said he was my boyfriend. He said this frequently, loudly, in front of the whole class. It shamed me, utterly.

Once Mrs. Pirelli made Ritchie and me team captains for kickball. We stood at the front of two lines of children, and Ritchie said, so everyone could hear, "Two lovebirds together." Without even thinking, I kicked him in the shin. Unfazed, he smiled at me and said, "A love tap from my girlfriend." My head spun in impotent rage.

At recess three times a day he chased me. The other two worst boys in our class, his friends, rode herd across the playground to help him corner, then catch, then kiss me. I spent many recesses trapped inside the girls' bathroom, the only safe spot. Even there, Ritchie and his friends taunted me from the doorway, slapping a foot over the threshold, threatening to come in, then jumping back again.

Sometimes Lisa spelled me. She'd put on my big blue fake suede coat, pull up the hood with the fake fur, and set off running. I'd wear her navy blue parka. For a while they'd be fooled and chase her. She ran fast, much faster than I did. They rarely caught her, and even when they did, when she turned around and peered at them through her thick brown frames, they peeled away, unwilling to kiss a girl with glasses.

Lisa Adelson and I had met the year before, thrown together as the only girls in our reading group in the second grade, and had been inseparable ever since. Lisa wore her straight brown hair in two high riding ponytails, gathered tight above either ear. She was skinnier and faster than I was, and she wore glasses. Otherwise we were the same. Her parents had been divorced since she was five. Now that I too packed a backpack on Fridays and went to my father's, we were even more closely bound.

We were in third grade now, and at least for me it was not going well. My teacher was tall and strict, and for the first time in my life I was not the pet. Everybody could read; I was no longer a prodigy. We were concentrating on penmanship instead, and my letters would not grow smooth and even like the script on the laminated sheets of paper over which we labored. Also, Mrs. Pirelli did not like it when I was late for school. I was late pretty much every day.

And then there was Ritchie, ever at my heels. At the end of each school day, Lisa and Laurie Mori escorted me from the schoolyard, two small bodyguards on either side of me. Ritchie and his friends followed, one step behind us, talking about us loudly, while we pretended they were not there. Laurie lived just a block up from me on 24th Avenue. I'd hide out at her house until Ritchie and his friends got bored waiting for me outside.

Something dark, something ugly was working its way over me, latching onto everything in my life. Those boys knew it. They smelled my fear, sensed my shame, knew I wouldn't have the guts to turn around and dare them to kiss me, knew I wouldn't have the confidence to go to a teacher for help, knew I'd make a perfect victim.

So I hunkered down and waited them out at Laurie's house, determined not to let them anywhere near my house, not to lead them straight into the core of my weakness.

At home my mother grew both vaguer and sharper. Her presence in the house shifted between a kind of vacant absence, when for hours at a time she was unaware of us, to an unshakable vigilance, when she required knowledge and control over the most minute details of our lives.

Though she was often unreachable, lost in reveries, communicating with presences we could not see, her illness did not bring on collapse. She never became an invalid, someone to be taken care of. Rather she pared down, whittled herself to a fearsome point. For the things that did concern her, she had an inexhaustible energy. Her authority over us grew with her illness. She occupied the center of my consciousness as surely and completely as she had in my early childhood, only now the central chord was dread, not wonder.

Her hands were still on the reins of the day-to-day workings of our lives. She deposited the rent checks, which the neighbors who were our tenants slipped under our door. When a tenant called to report a leak, she got a plumber. She paid the mortgage each month. When people moved out of the building she painted apartments, placed ads in the paper, and rented them out. She still made lunches and got us off to school. To the outside world she appeared normal, or normal enough. She never really lost her grasp on reality, in the sense that she always understood how other people would see her. Her paranoia was self-protective; to the uninitiated she kept mum about her true purpose on this earth.

When summer ended, she began to leave the house again. Done erasing the past, she now had business to attend to in the world. She'd take the station wagon—which had collected parking tickets on the windshield all summer and miraculously had not been towed—and go to the grocery store, or the bank, or to the fabric store to buy more patterns and polyester print fabrics for the tops and pants she sewed for us. Sometimes she'd be gone for hours at a time, and we had no idea where she was or when she'd be home.

When she went out, she no longer wore dresses or skirts or high-heeled pumps. She'd shed femininity and sexuality along with marriage and domesticity, adopting a uniform of her own—baggy polyester pants with elastic waistbands and plain blouses on top—in dark colors: navy blue, hunter green, and gray.

Amy and I still liked to rummage through her deep walk-in closet and play dress-up. We'd work our way through the hangers and piles of old clothes on the floor—short, tight, 60s-style dresses with A-line skirts in funny swirling oranges and greens—clothes from the days when my parents went out every Saturday night, my mother in black patent leather heels, a blue dress that came just above her knees, and an onyx brooch set in curling silver at her throat.

The sky blue wool coat with white rabbit cuffs and collars that my father used to help her into still hung in the back of the closet. If I pressed my cheek to the sleeve, ran my nose over the soft fur of the cuff, I could still catch a whiff of my parents' romance, could imagine my mother stepping down the stairs of her hotel in Paris. That was the woman I aspired to be, even if she no longer did.

She took to wearing a beige-colored trench coat whenever she left the house. Summer, winter, spring, and fall, that coat covered her body, muffled her shape, and redefined who she was. That coat loomed across the playground when she came to pick me up from school. It was instantly recognizable as she rounded the corner of our block. It harbored anger in its folds. It flapped in the wind. That coat made scenes wherever it went.

A woman in a trench coat, with graying hair of a certain length, can still make my heart stop—perhaps because my mother always wore the coat in public, and it was in public that she was most damaging. On the city bus I sat next to her. She laughed out loud. At nothing—or something that came from the inside. People on the bus turned to look. The pressure of their eyes on my skin exhausted me. The gaze of a woman across from us passed over my mother, then rested on me. I had a choice—look the other way and pretend not to be a part of her, or move closer and try to make it look as if we were talking, as if something I said made her laugh. Own her or disown her.

In the Tea Garden we came upon two teenage girls with long hair and thin faces, wading in the pool under the wooden bridge. Feet bare, pants rolled to their knees, they were scavenging coins from the bottom of the pond. People strolling through the garden turned their heads to follow the girls with their eyes as they passed, but no one said anything.

My mother stopped dead in her tracks. She watched for a moment, her face stiff, her lips drawn in. She moved in towards the girls suddenly, leaving me holding Amy's hand on the stone path that traversed the water. The girls turned; they could feel her coming.

"What do you think you're doing?" she asked, her voice sharp and staccato. They stared back, blank and stunned. "Get out of that pond," she yelled with enough menace to bring them out fast. They grabbed their shoes, not looking up at the small crowd that had now gathered around us. They pulled their socks on over wet feet. My mother stood over them.

"You should be ashamed of yourselves," she said.

The girls fled, edging past Amy and me, frozen on the narrow bridge. I wanted to sink into stone. One of them turned as she passed me, her long straw-colored hair rising and falling on her back. "Fuckin' crazy," she muttered.

I looked to my mother. She stood steady, stalking the girls

with her gaze as they went, her coat billowing behind her in the afternoon wind.

At school we read the story of the Five Chinese Brothers. Each of the brothers had a special power. The first brother could swallow the ocean. He knelt down on the shore, and in one long gulp he drank the water. When he stood up, his head was huge and wobbly-looking on top of his thin body. From the picture you could see how hard his cheeks were straining, pulling at the seams, the way they do when you try to hold in a big gulp of air. He sent a little boy out to gather all the fish flopping on the exposed sand. The boy walked farther and farther out. Maybe he got greedy, or maybe each time he was about to turn around and go back to shore, he saw one more thing he wanted, a lobster scuttling over the sand, an abalone shell iridescent in the sun. The first brother waved his arms in the air, but the boy could not see him. He couldn't yell—his mouth was full of ocean. He wobbled back and forth, nearly toppling under the weight of his big head. Finally he burst.

"It is hard," the book said, "to hold back the ocean."

In the aftermath of our trip to Clear Lake, my father got a restraining order prohibiting my mother from taking us outside the city of San Francisco. This, like the divorce papers, arrived in the mail, and like the divorce papers it sent my mother into a rage.

Perhaps that's what set her off. Or maybe it was something else entirely—some minor infraction of the rules committed over a weekend visit to my father's—that made her yell at Sara and me. All I know for sure is that Sara's guitar was leaning against the wall by the piano in the front hallway. My mother reached for it, wrapped her fists tight around its neck. She lifted the guitar high above her head and brought it smashing down into the wall. The amber frame crushed into the hollow interior. The strings howled as they snapped. The smell of splintered wood bit the air. My mother stayed in motion, too fast to track, plumbing between walls. Standing tall, lifting what was left of the guitar, she brought it crashing down again and again and again into the doorjamb. When she was done, she clutched six inches of guitar neck in her hand. The metal strings, still wound tight round the tuning keys, hung loose like severed veins.

I was very still—breath hard in my chest, straining to my throat as I watched and waited to see if she was done, ears perked, every muscle straining to the noise, fingers and toes slightly numb from the blood pulsing into them.

Did she stalk away? Run from the house? Retreat to her bedroom convulsed by sobs? Perhaps she sat in silence in the big chair at the head of the dining room table, so that none of us could move. I didn't know if it was over, or if she was just pausing for breath. I was fixed in place for an hour, for two hours, waiting to see if she would rise again, my body still, my heart noisy against my eardrums, long after my breathing returned to normal.

Maybe that day with the guitar it was like this: She went to the kitchen. She made toasted cheese sandwiches in the electric griddle. She called us in for dinner and we ate, together, in blistered silence.

Once she threw her purse through the living room window. I didn't see the window break, but she sent me to retrieve the purse from the front yard. I crept through the bushes, under the acacia tree, where shards of glass were buried in the deep green ivy. The purse was white. I was wearing my tennis shoes without socks. I was afraid I would step on glass. I was even more afraid someone would see me.

Less than every day, but more than once a month, my mother tore up the house. She broke windows, battered walls, scarred furniture. Amy would hide under my bed. Or both of us would hide in the deep walk-in closet off our bedroom, listening, on our knees, following my mother's heavy footfall through the apartment, and then the sound of things shattering. (Dishes against the wall? The iron through a window? An upholstered seat ripped loose from a dining room chair flung against a mirror?)

Over time her rage shifted from the inanimate objects in the house to my sister Sara, who, with each passing day, was drawn deeper and deeper into conflict with my mother. Sara, who was twelve, thirteen, then fourteen, running through her shoes, becoming lanky and curvy all at once, painfully aware of how awkward she looked in the clothes my mother sewed for us, chafing at the regulation of our lives. Sara, who'd come up in easier times and lacked the instinct for dissembling that Amy and I quickly acquired. Sara, who stumbled again and again into my mother's fury unwary and undefended. Sara, whose body stretched inexorably towards womanhood, filled with the threat and promise of sexuality, which seemed in itself an affront to my mother. She would have kept us all small, towed behind her by the invisible string of her will, like the baby ducks in the Tea Garden, knowing nothing but their mother's wake. Sara would not stop growing.

My parents met once a month or so—someplace neutral—to talk about finances, our progress in school, or perhaps just so my father could take her temperature. My mother could be quite civil, attending to the business side of our lives undisturbed. And maybe she had her own strategic reasons for meeting with him. Keeping an eye on the enemy.

Once, late in the school year, they met at a coffee shop across the street from his office on Union Street. They talked calmly for an hour or so, and then as my father prepared to leave, he reached into his suit pocket for a pen to write out the alimony/child support check. He pulled out a Cross pen that Sadie, my mother's mother, had given him as a present years before. My mother recognized it at once and snatched it from him. Why did he still have it? Did he carry it every day? Did he keep it close to his heart? He asked her why it mattered. She said his carrying the pen was bad for Sadie.

"Why?" my father pressed.

She took a napkin from the dispenser on the table and drew a line with the pen across the middle. On top of the line she wrote *Laura, Amy, Sadie*. Under the line she wrote *Russell* and *Amos*. Then, *Sara*.

My father stared at the napkin.

"Why is Sara below the line?"

"She's crossed over," my mother said. "She's with you. She may as well be dead to me."

Then she got up, put the pen in the pocket of her beige overcoat, and walked out of the coffee shop.

My father was stunned. He'd known that eventually he would have to sue for custody. He'd delayed because taking us away from her seemed too cruel. She'd already lost so much—he felt losing us would remove her last anchor to reality. Without us, he thought, she'd slip away completely into her own world. He'd never imagined that my mother would turn on one of us.

He walked back across the street to his office, jaywalking in front of traffic. He picked up the phone, called the lawyer who had handled the divorce case, and asked him to begin custody proceedings against my mother.

Chapter Ten

I DON'T REMEMBER when or how my father told us he was suing for custody, only that this pending decision, attached to the word *custody*, hung over us for a very long time. The possibility of leaving my mother would never have occurred to me. In all her strangeness, violence, and chaos, my mother was my life. How could that change? But once my father raised the possibility of a different life, I began to hold the possibility in my mind, and everything shifted. My father trying to get us, my mother violently opposed, became the framework for our lives for two and a half years. At some point a decision would be handed down. But the when and the how of it was a moving target, the subject for me of constant fantasy and fear.

For Easter my father took us to Lake Tahoe for a week. His new girlfriend, who worked at his real estate office, came with us. We'd met Jeni before on weekend outings—gone for dinner at her apartment, eyed her cautiously, quietly pushed the onions she put in the spaghetti sauce to the side of the plate (my mother did not put onions in spaghetti sauce), and remained painfully polite. On this trip to Tahoe we got to know her better. Each day we all went sledding on a huge hill near Lake Tahoe. That hill has long since been closed to sledding—a lawsuit waiting to happen. But in the less litigious days of the 1970s my father was a demon on the toboggan. Against all reason we felt safe, as long as he was the one steering.

In a series of pictures from this trip my sisters and I stand in rubber boots, three feet deep in snow, triumphantly wielding huge icicles we've wedged loose from the eaves. We look a little raggedy, in too-short bell-bottom pants and funny belted coats (the same blue faux-suede one I traded with Lisa at school). But then everyone's photos from the 1970s look like this. We are also—children in the snow—undeniably happy.

The strongest image I carry from that trip is not captured in a photo. My sisters and I ran into the cabin one afternoon after hours in the snow, legs and butts frozen, wool gloves soggy, and found that Jeni had hot chocolate waiting for us in the kitchen. She'd set out cookies. On a plate. It was almost too much to take in—utterly seductive, like something off TV. The way children and mothers were supposed to be. How could I resist?

I began to hold images in my mind's eye: clean sheets, the dark indigo of store-bought blue jeans, the gleaming surfaces of clean kitchen appliances, chocolate chip cookies on a plate. Of course I wanted to live with my father. What was not possible to imagine was how this might be achieved, the means by which I would be severed from my mother.

When summer came my mother again promised we would go to Colorado for the Barton family reunion. Each week she spoke with her parents by phone, and each week she assured them we would come this year, but she'd made no signs of preparations for a trip.

She did get out of the house more that summer. Refugees from Vietnam were arriving by the planeload at the military base in the Presidio—a stone's throw from our house. My mother followed the war intently to its bitter end. We'd all watched TV together as those last helicopters took off from the roof of the embassy in Saigon earlier in the spring. My mother was so affected by those images that she offered herself up as a volunteer at Letterman Hospital, which was a reception center for arriving Vietnamese orphans. Given how erratic she was at home, it is hard to imagine how she pulled this off, but she did, coming home with stories of holding Vietnamese babies in her arms.

My sisters and I, under very loose supervision, ranged farther and farther from home. I had Lisa to play with, and most days we'd meet up somewhere between my house and hers. Or Sara and Amy and Lisa's sister Naomi joined us—Lisa's mother entrusted Sara, who was now twelve, to keep an eye on all of us. We'd walk down to Baker Beach, a few blocks from our house, to play in the surf.

In her flurry of activity my mother took us to a series of county fairs—to Sonoma and Napa and all the way to Sacramento for the state fair. We went on roller coasters, looked at prize pigs, and attended the inevitable country music concerts that were probably what drew my mother in the first place. I remember a singer in a short white suede dress and cowboy boots—I want to say it was Tammy Wynette, but I can't be sure—singing in an outdoor amphitheater with lots of hay bales and the certain feeling that we did not belong there.

For my ninth birthday my mother organized a party for me. The apartment across the hall was vacant (and clean), so we had the party there. I was able to invite friends over for the first time in years. My mother baked an angel food cake and decorated it to look like a carnival carousel. She used a Japanese paper umbrella for the roof, held in place by red and white straws. Animal crackers stood in a circle on top of the white frosting—the horses and animals on the ride. It was the most charming cake I had ever seen—have ever seen—which is to say that, even then, my mother could still summon her former magic. She made a pin-the-tale-on-the-donkey set from scratch, and we all played games and ate cake in the empty apartment. Even my father came, with gifts—six brand-new T-shirts, one of which said, "I'm a women's libber." My mother was brittle and suspicious whenever my father was around, but she let him stay for cake. She took away most of the T-shirts after he left, but she let me keep the women's libber one.

One weekend towards the end of summer, my father picked us up and announced as he pulled away from the curb that we were going out of town the next day.

"Where?"

"It's a surprise."

"Tahoe?"

"No."

"Yosemite?"

"You'll find out tomorrow."

"Does Mom know?"

"Don't worry."

I felt the bottom of my stomach lift from its pilings. Sara turned to me from the front seat, and our eyes met in alarm.

My father drove us to the Sears on Geary Boulevard to buy some clothes for the trip. "Pick out whatever you want, enough for a few days," he said. We looked nervously at one another. We hadn't been in a department store in two years, and my mother never let us choose our own clothes.

My father pulled a red and white pair of shorts with a matching red halter top off the rack. "How about this?" Sara and I exchanged looks again. Even if she'd let us buy clothes, she'd never let us wear a halter top, not in a million years. "Try it on," he said, handing me the hanger.

We loosened up soon enough, and each of us carried a bagful of forbidden clothes back to my father's apartment, waiting to see what act of open revolt would follow.

When we got on 101 South the next morning, we realized we were headed to the airport.

"Are we going to Denver?" I asked in amazement.

My father nodded.

"Mom doesn't know?" Sara asked.

"I'll call her after we get there. You guys can tell her I didn't tell you where you were going."

"You're kidnapping us?" Sara said.

My father laughed. "That's right, I've kidnapped you."

And then we were all laughing, nervous and excited—a week with our cousins whom we hadn't seen in years, new clothes, an airplane ride, this dangerous but fun complicity with my father—and sick to our stomachs—god only knew what hell we'd pay when we got home.

In Denver my father rented a car and called my grandparents from the airport. He hadn't said a word to them ahead of time because he didn't want them to alert my mother. They were so shocked and upset about being forced into open conflict with my mother, they almost didn't want us to come.

My father stayed only one night. His intention had been to deliver us to Denver in time for the family reunion, which was to be held up in the mountains later in the week. He thought that after being promised this trip so many times, we needed to go. He also wanted to have a face-to-face conversation with my grandparents.

My grandmother made fried chicken for dinner and baked us a pie. She was thrilled to see us, even though she did not like crossing my mother this way. We had corn fresh from the garden. Amos always grew his own, even in the bone-dry Denver suburb where they now lived. "If you trip on the way in from the garden, the corn's not fresh enough anymore," he said.

At the table we all joined hands, while Amos said a solemn lengthy grace. He thanked the lord for our presence with them and then asked the lord to watch over Sally, who couldn't be with us tonight. When he mentioned my mother, my sisters and I twitched in our seats.

During dinner my father pressed my grandfather, asking him to play a more active role in urging my mother to get treatment. Amos bristled. Sadie was near tears. By now they must have known that my father was right.

"Russ, let's not discuss this in front of the children," Amos said.

I looked from my father to my grandfather. Amos's white head was bent over his plate. He forced us all into silence with his solemnity. Even my father had had to bow his head in grace. I felt a flash of anger towards Amos. Not talk about Mom in front of us? We lived with her. Did he think we hadn't noticed?

After dinner Amos phoned my mother from his office in the basement. My sisters and I waited upstairs for the verdict. We were terrified he would send us back right away—before the reunion, before we could see our cousins or wear our new clothes. Our return was inevitable, her fury was inevitable; we pinned our hopes on putting it off as long as possible. My mother, of course, wanted us home immediately. She had custody of us—my father had no legal right to take us. Amos nearly gave in. Under extreme pressure from my father, he did let us stay, but only for four days, not the full week my father had planned. My mother also extracted a promise from Amos not to take us to the mountains. She had a bad feeling about the mountains.

After Amos finished I sat in the huge black leather chair

behind his desk and heard my mother's voice, panicky and wired, come across the line. "You're going to come home on Tuesday," she was saying. "You're not going to go to the mountains," she was telling me, as if to reassure herself. My father's taking us away had caught her completely off guard. She wasn't even mad, just desperate for us to come home.

For our sake, the family reunion was held early in the city at my grandparents' house. All fifteen grandchildren slept over— lined up in sleeping bags on the floor of the living room. We played pool tournaments and foosball in the basement. Our cousins taught us how to play kick-the-can, which consumed our days and evenings. We wore the halter tops and brightly colored shorts, knowing they would disappear as soon as we got home, and roamed through the brand-new, sparsely popu- lated subdivision like prisoners on leave, exhilarated and taut, knowing the string that attached us to my mother would snap back hard when we got home.

As it turned out, our return was rather uneventful. My father picked us up at the airport, and we drove home with increas- ing dread. Once we got inside, my mother was extra-glad to see us, hugging and kissing us, keeping us close that day. She wasn't angry with us at all. My father had effectively taken all the blame. For once she didn't even want to hear about what we'd done while we were gone. We were bursting with stories to tell her about our cousins and our grandparents' new home. She didn't ask. In fact, she seemed to want to pretend the whole thing had never happened.

So there was no great scene. Just a makeshift dinner of

creamed tuna on toast, the stale smell of the apartment, the country music on the radio, and our own homemade clothes to welcome us back.

The next year—fourth grade—I didn't make it to school every day. The alarm clock would go off in the bedroom, and my mother would call to me to get in bed with her. Sara, in junior high now, was out the door before I ever got up. Amy, now in first grade, could sleep a little longer since her elementary school was nearby. I had to catch a school bus two blocks away for an interminable ride across town.

When I got in bed with my mother, she would wrap her legs around me and ask about my dreams. The white numbers on the clock radio by her bedside flipped along until it was too late to make the bus.

"I'll drive you to school," she'd say, or "I'll write you a note if you're late." She searched for the car keys, while I dragged a brush over the tangles in my hair.

Outside the schoolyard, I sat in the passenger seat, unable to open the door of the Oldsmobile. The car smelled like sour milk. The sight of the empty schoolyard filled me with shame. I had to cross that yard and then the silent hallways, skulking along, late, moving quickly, praying I would not cross paths with anyone. I'd go up the staircase, down the long hall to my classroom. When I opened the door, thirty-five pairs of eyes would fix on me. I'd have to put my coat in the closet while they all watched, and weave my way through the maze of desks to my spot up front. I sat near the chalkboard so I could see. For two years now, after I failed the eye test at school, the nurse had sent me home with a note for my mother saying I needed glasses. My mother took the notes, but did not take me to the eye doctor.

Lisa would smile when she saw me. I would tuck my books into the space under the desk and only then, slowly, as the class resumed, would I fold back into anonymity.

"You don't have to go. I'll write you a note."

On those days, instead of going to school my mother would take Amy—who made it to school even less than I did—and me to Golden Gate Park to our old haunts at the Tea Garden or across the Bay to Mount Tamalpais. My mother had taken up photography. She used my father's old Nikon. She developed the photos herself. I suppose she must have taken classes. Somewhere in the city there was a darkroom where she went to work while we were at school or in the afternoons when she left us alone. It seems implausible now that she did this, had the wherewithal, the focus, to learn something as new and technical as photography. But I have the photos, glossy black-and-whites of Amy and me in the Botanical Gardens—just across the way from the Tea Garden in the park. Amy looks happy. Her hand reaches out to toss a crust of bread to a white swan. She is much too close to it. I'm in the background, awkward in a dark blue coat, a miniature version of my mother's trench coat. I'm only nine, but already you can see in the slump of my shoulders, in the refusal to muster a real smile, in my utter self-consciousness, how unwilling I am to be there.

Mount Tam smelled of eucalyptus and bay laurels. We collected bay leaves off the ground to put in spaghetti sauce at home. My mother put little black briquettes in the grill to cook hot dogs, but she didn't light them. On these trips she always forgot something, like lighter fluid or the hot dogs, and we were always hungry long before the food was ready.

Mount Tam was deserted. Everyone else was where they were supposed to be, at work or at school. Amy and I lodged our tiny cans of grape juice in the stream that trickled down the mountain, so they'd be cold when we wanted to drink them. The branches of the live oaks curled up through the sun. Tall straight Douglas firs thrust up through the jumble. Long curling moss hung off the trees.

"It's an enchanted forest," I said to Amy, looking around, casting my plot. "And you have to cross the bridge."

My mother sat quietly at the picnic table, her hands cupped before her on the table, watching the water flow over the rocks.

I crawled down under the wooden bridge that crossed the steam and squatted on a rock. The rushing water threw up a chill that soaked me.

Amy walked over the bridge. I called out, "Who's that walking over my bridge?"

A laugh came from my mother's direction. Amy turned to look.

"Don't look," I whispered. Amy's lips puckered up in hurt. I resumed my troll voice. "Ay, my pretty, don't look away. You can't escape me," I said. She giggled and fell back into the game.

We took off our shoes, rolled up our pant legs and dipped our feet, wrinkled from our sweaty socks, into the water. The rocks were sharp as we hopped back and forth, shouting at our bravery and the cold.

Late in the afternoon, when we were hungry, I went over and sat on the bench next to my mother. She didn't stir. I traced lines into the surface of the picnic table, the soft wood giving easily under my fingernail. My mother was still, gazing out at nothing. I tried to look where she was looking and saw a shaft of sunlight filled with gnats and mosquitoes. Redwood trees channeled light up their trunks. Spiders traced the lateral spaces between the trees. Flies flickered in and out of shadow, visible to us for only seconds. Memory works like this, tossing you a shimmering detail, but holding whole seasons of your life in shade.

"Mommy," I murmured, "shouldn't we light the charcoals?"

She started. "We're going to in just a sec, sweetie." We sat there together in silence for several more minutes, watching the bugs dance in the light.

Finally she roused herself and lit the charcoal with bits of paper we tore from a brown paper grocery bag. Amy and I ate oranges while we waited for the coals to get hot.

On the way back down to the parking lot, I slipped crossing the stream and soaked one foot. My tennis shoe slogged along, leaving a single set of wet footprints on the trail all the way down to the car.

Near the parking lot we ran into a ranger. He was the first person we'd seen all day.

"How are you ladies doing?" he asked in a friendly way that I knew would rile my mother.

She paused—too long—then said, "We're just fine," in the curt voice she used with strangers.

The ranger looked at her a long moment from under his hat. He glanced at Amy. She smiled back at him. She could always charm strangers, and remained open and unguarded long after Sara and I had become wary. I shuffled my wet foot in the dirt. "You ladies have a nice day," he said, and walked away. His glance seared me. I knew what he was thinking. *Why isn't she at school?*

In the car Amy wanted to sing. I pushed her away and leaned my head down on the open window frame to let the wind rake me. I watched the trees fly by until looking at them gave me a physical nausea to match my mood. Days like this would lead only one place: to picnic tables and park benches in the middle of the day, when everyone else was in school or working. I'd be the grown-up, staring at bugs, laughing out loud when nobody was there and nothing was funny.

There were many days like that. Days of sun or fog when I stayed home with my mother or we roamed the city, making pilgrimages to JFK Drive and watching the ducklings come of age each spring in the Tea Garden. My mother told me things. She told me that she watched the Lawrence Welk show each night at seven, not because she loved polkas but because there was a girl in the chorus who looked like me. Every good person who watched helped me be good; the bad ones pulled me onto the bad side. My mother watched for me.

She told me that the drought we were experiencing was a good thing. "Normally the bad side has control of the weather," she explained. "Lately the good side is doing better; that's why we have this drought." The whole state was on voluntary water rationing, yet my mother would leave the faucet in the kitchen sink on full blast all afternoon and sometimes she put the garden hose in the bushes and left that running too, at a trickle, overnight. The neighbors were not pleased, but I think they were too intimidated by my mother to say anything. I figured this was her way of helping the drought along. It made sense. Everything she said made sense in a way. There was a pattern to it, and if I could get a handle on it, map it all out, I'd be safe. I'd be able to manage her, keep her from getting mad, or at least keep her from getting mad at me. Up to now her fury had been directed at my father, at presences I could not see, at the walls and furniture of the house, and more and more at Sara, but so far not at me.

Amy and I had a new plotline for our dolls. It involved a voyage to Europe, a shipboard romance, trunks of clothes, a young woman away from home for the first time. For romances we held the dolls' faces together, pressed lip to molded-plastic lip, the way people kissed in the old black-and-white movies we watched on TV on Saturdays.

This plot too was drawn from the pages of a book—Amy's trip to Europe with Aunt March in *Little Women*. In our version that boat set sail a hundred times, streamers unfurled from the side of our bunk bed, a young woman standing at the railing—but I don't think it ever arrived. It's only now that I realize the obvious—that Amy and I were faithfully reenacting my mother's voyage of 1960, bringing a more attractive version of her back to life. What part of my mother's story did I imprint on my own imagination as we played? Is it my mother standing at the rail, or is it Jo in her long blue dress? Is it 1960 or 1860?

Sometimes I played with Jo alone. She stood with her arms out and to the sides a little, wavering there as if she were trying to keep her balance. On her fingers there were tiny plastic ridges that looked just like knuckles. I would try to wrap her stiff arms around her dance partner and spin them together as if they were one thing, but Jo wouldn't cling to her partners. She put her arms out when she twirled, to feel the air rushing through her outspread fingers, the same way I did when I spun in the living room, twirling faster and faster, holding my arms out against the force that pushed them in, until I collapsed in a breathless heap on the still-spinning floor.

Sara did not play dolls with us anymore. She was always angling to get out of the house now, over to a friend's to play. She'd bought a Barbie with her own money and she kept it at her friend Nancy's house. Nancy had a whole collection of Barbies—Ken, Skipper, the camper, the works.

Sometimes, Sara smuggled her Barbie into our apartment, inside a sock, in a shoebox, in her backpack. She and I played with it in the bathroom off her bedroom, the most remote spot in the house from my mother. She had to come through Sara's room to find us, and we could hear her coming.

When we weren't playing with it, Sara put the Barbie back in the sock, in the shoebox in the back of her closet. My mother found it anyway. She had a nose for these things, a Geiger counter for the toxic objects we brought into the house. I ran out to the hallway when I heard my mother screaming, but froze when I saw her. She had the Barbie in one fist, Sara's hair in the other. I couldn't see Sara's face—it was blocked by my mother's body—but I heard her shriek, an incoherent, "I didn't mean to, I didn't mean to." My mother shook Sara by the shoulders, shoved her against the wall. Small bruises, the size of my mother's fingers, appeared on Sara's upper arms the next day. She slammed Sara into the wall, and I heard my sister's jaw rattle. "Do you think you can hide things from me?" my mother was asking. "I am your mother." She raised the Barbie in the air and swiped its rubbery legs across my sister's face.

Chapter Eleven

MY FATHER FILED for full custody of my sisters and me in the summer of 1975. His suit did not go before a judge until the fall of 1976, a full year and a half later.

Finally, in preparation for the hearing, during the fall of fifth grade, the child welfare department sent a social worker out to visit. He was supposed to speak to all the parties involved, observe the home, and make his recommendation to the court.

My mother prepared for him. We helped her clear a path—right down our old running track—through the long front hall, past the piano, to the couches in the living room. The doors along the hallway—to the bedrooms and the kitchen—were pushed closed, and everything that might have blocked his path we piled behind them. The dining room, which opened to the living room and could not be concealed, we arranged so that it looked clean as long as you didn't get too close. We transferred everything from the dining room table—the sewing machine and all the material and patterns, plus all the bills, papers, and books that had settled in on top of that—to the floor of my mother's bedroom. The back hallway was so crowded with all the mail and newspapers we'd lugged from the living room and front hall that Sara could barely get in and out of her bedroom. The back door was impassable. All the junk on top of the coffee tables and the parquet floor in the dining room we scooped up and jammed into the drawers of the buffet in the dining room, flattening them out so the drawers closed. Our stuff—clothes, games, toys, and books, which had spread throughout the house—we shoved into the large walk-in closet in the bedroom I shared with Amy.

When my mother swept the front hall and living room, the vacuum cleaner heaved and rattled, choking on tacks, coins, rubber bands, on two years of debris, but somehow got the job done. After, the sight of our naked, sky blue carpets, the ones that had seemed so open and limitless just four years before when we moved in, shocked us. The vacuuming revealed ugly spots, oily and coarse, brown stains in the carpets that would not come out. We pushed the couches and armchairs and throw rug around as best we could to cover them. Then we waited in the unfamiliar clean of the living room for the man from child welfare to arrive.

Mr. Judson sat at one end of the green sofa, looking down though his glasses at a sheaf of papers he'd taken from his black briefcase. I don't remember if he asked to see the rest of the house—our bedrooms, the kitchen. Surely the jig would have been up if he'd seen the kitchen. My mother would have headed off any suggestion of a full tour. She had a way of foreclosing certain lines of conversation.

He was round and middle-aged. His suit—perhaps it had fit better a few years earlier—made it difficult for him to get comfortable on the sofa. I sat at the other end, backed all the way up to the arm, so that I could feel the bones of the sofa through the upholstery hard against my back. I hugged a small cushion to my stomach and traced the spiraling pattern on its fabric as I waited for him to speak. My mother hadn't coached us on what to say, but she stood, I assumed, just behind the closed door in the hallway, listening. The way Sara remembers it, my mother stayed even closer, in the dining room, where she could follow every word.

Mr. Judson shifted and settled, then finally drew a steno pad from his briefcase, lowered his horn-rimmed glasses on his nose and looked down at me over the rims. I tried to keep my index finger on the outside of the green paisley design and follow the swirls in and out. Each time the pattern would switch, and my finger would end up on the inside again. Mr. Judson smiled and asked a few questions about school, my grades, my friends. I told him my teacher's name was Mrs. Collins, and my best friend's name was Lisa, and I had just been put in gifted. He nodded. Preliminaries.

Then he shifted gears. "You should feel free to tell me anything you want. Neither your Mom or Dad is going to know what you say, so don't worry about that. OK?" He pointed a trained look of concern at me over the glasses.

"OK," I whispered, hoping he would take my cue and lower his voice.

"Where do you like it better, at your mother's house, or your father's house?"

I looked down, pressing my nail into the green tapestry of the pillow. I wanted to tell him that I wanted to live with my father. I intended to tell him this. But I felt the question had to be answered exactly the way he'd posed it.

"I like it at my father's," I said, looking up at him. "It's very clean."

He nodded, wrote something down.

"I like it here too," I said, looking down again. I paused, shifting my eyes to the dining room. "There's some problems." Tears welled in my eyes, but I thought I could manage them. I took a breath, searching for words. Even under less stressful circumstances it took me time to gather my words.

"I understand, this is very difficult," Mr. Judson said, interrupting my thoughts. "You love both your Mom and your Dad."

"Yeah," I whispered. True enough, though hardly the point.

"There're some problems," I ventured again, hoping to stir his interest.

"I understand. Every family has problems. You know," he said, as if the thought had just occurred to him, "you don't have to choose between your Dad or Mom." I looked back at him, eyebrows knit. Of course I had to choose—that was the whole point, wasn't it?

He reached into his briefcase, drew out a small pack of Kleenex, and handed me a tissue. I wiped my eyes, and he made more notes on his steno pad. I tried out sentences in my head: *My mother is not very well. My mother gets very angry sometimes. My mother gets very angry with my sister sometimes.* Ever polite, I waited for him to finish writing.

He looked up at me suddenly, "OK then, I'll talk to your sister now," he looked back down at his notebook, "Sara. Would you go get Sara for me?"

I sat there a second while he looked at me expectantly. "OK," I said, slowly moving the cushion from my lap. I stood up, glanced back at him once, confused and shamed, knowing I had muffed it somehow, had lacked the nerve to do what needed to be done. I could only hope Sara would do better.

Several weeks later my mother held up a thick sheaf of legal papers, folded over four times. "This is the court's decision," she said.

I sat at the foot of her bed, my heart pounding. She sat above me, Indian-style, among the swirling sheets and blankets on her single bed, which was pushed up against the wall. All the junk from the dining room was still in there, so it was crowded on the floor. And dim, as the shades were always drawn. I couldn't see her face clearly.

"It says that Sara and Amy want to live with their mother, and Laura could not decide." I did not dare look at her, but my neck hunched down between my shoulders as I waited for the fury that must surely finally be unleashed on me. She went on, almost without missing a beat. "They made a mistake; they got your name mixed up with Sara's."

She continued to leaf through the pages, not even looking to me for confirmation. I didn't offer any. Just sat there on the floor, feeling the moment mow me down. Mown like that, I couldn't correct her, could only watch mutely as the moment passed. There was time enough to calculate that this, like everything else, would not go down easily for Sara, time enough to take in something I had already intuited: if you say nothing, people assume you are on their side.

In bed that night, finally away from my mother, my disappointment bore down hard. The judge had granted my mother full custody, based on the recommendation of Mr. Judson. My father retained weekend visitation rights, but that was all—we were not going to live with him. We were going to stay right here, in this mess with my mother. This reality was so wide, and heavy, so unexpected, I didn't think I could withstand it. For months now my existence had been rooted in the belief that everything around me was temporary, that another future, free of my mother's stifling presence, a future of clean carpets and dinners on the table every night, was coming. Holding that future in my mind was what made it possible to get through the days.

The television crackled in the other room. I could hear the hollow sound of laughter—my mother watching Johnny Carson do his nightly monologue. The sheets felt hot; I knew I wouldn't sleep.

And what about Sara? She wanted to live with my father even more than I did. Why hadn't she told Mr. Judson the truth? At least I'd stuck my neck out a little—and for what? I was furious at her. I couldn't be furious at her. She hadn't said anything, and she was still the one in trouble over what I'd said.

I was furious at my father too. He'd been so sure. Now he'd lost. He'd promised we would live with him. Promised things would change and soon. I'd counted on his ability to know the future. What did he know? It felt like the floor falling out of the earth. Maybe he didn't know anything; maybe he wasn't stronger than my mother. And yet I could no more be mad at him than I could be at Sara. He was my only lifeline.

So I focused on Mr. Judson. A pure and uncomplicated hatred for him carried me through the dark hours of the night. He'd promised me my mother would not find out what I told him. Then he'd written it all down and mailed her a copy. He must have known he was going to do that all along and lied just to get me to talk.

At some point as I lay on my stomach in bed, I steepled my hands together, leaned them against the bedstead, and addressed my words to God. I told him my story. I began as far back as I could remember. How we'd moved to this apartment and my mother had changed. How *He* needed to help her. But most of all, how *He* needed to help me go live with my father. I listed my complaints. The mess covering all the floors, which surely God in his heaven could see. That she talked with devils. That she got very angry. Wouldn't let us leave the house. How everyone was afraid of her—my grandfather, my teachers at school, the neighbors, people in stores and on the street.

And somewhere in that night, when I had exhausted myself in tears and words, I felt calm, the cathartic release of confession, felt the sense of a sympathetic presence listening in the night. And finally I slept.

In the days that followed, on the bus to school or sitting by the window in the living room reading, when my eyes drifted up from my book to check the progress of the fog up the Bay, my thoughts would turn to escape by way of disaster. Fire. Flood. Earthquake. Something powerful that could wreck the house and force us to leave. Kidnapping. Especially kidnapping. Patty Hearst, who'd been taken from her dorm room at Berkeley just across the Bay, filled our imaginations. Images of her kidnapping played over and over in my mind, though of course there was no actual footage. Then I'd imagine my own mother standing in front of a row of microphones, wearing her trench coat and big black glasses to hide her tears like Mrs. Hearst. Here the fantasy faltered. My mother would be more angry than sad. She'd say something not right to the reporters, something no one would understand. They'd get the sharpness, though—the fury barely contained under her coat. Everyone would look around, embarrassed. *Jesus, we didn't kidnap her daughter*, they'd think. Not my mother, though; she'd keep eyeing them with her perfect knowledge of their complicity. She'd ruin the whole thing.

Chapter Twelve

MY FATHER SAT on the blue corduroy sofa in the front room of his apartment, his long legs reaching easily to the floor. I sat across from him on a wide green armchair, one he had dragged from 24th Avenue, and then to each of the three different apartments he'd lived in since he moved out, until he finally settled here on Jackson Street. It was Sunday afternoon, and my father and I were having one of many long conversations we would have in this room. I was ten years old.

"What does it mean?" I asked him, squinting, trying to bring the word into focus. He had to repeat "schizophrenia" several times before I could pronounce it. It was long and strange and frankly ugly. Even so, I had a feeling it was something I could hang onto, something I could rebuild my world around.

"It means someone can't tell the difference between what's real and what's not."

I nodded. Yes, that was it. "She talks to devils," I said, "to JFK."

He nodded sharply. I could see he didn't want to hear anymore. He wasn't fascinated by the details as I was. He'd put up a wall against my mother's internal world a long time ago. Instead, he told me about the disease.

I was taken with the comforting illusion that if you can name something, you understand it. That if you can name something, you're close to controlling it. And, most definitely, that if you can name something, you are no longer part of it. My mother couldn't tell the difference between what was real and what wasn't, but I could. Here I was, talking with my father like a grownup, planted firmly on his side of sanity, even if my feet didn't yet reach the floor. Schizophrenia: that word clanked like a prison door being pulled shut behind me. I was getting out; my mother wasn't.

"There are several different kinds of schizophrenia," he said. "Your mother's a paranoid schizophrenic."

Paranoid was a word I already knew. The two words together were doubly ugly.

Not knowing she was sick was one of the symptoms. Thinking everyone was fighting against her was another. So were hearing voices, being disorganized, and being angry.

"The only way for me to win custody of you guys is for me to prove that your mother is an unfit parent. That means putting this all out there. I didn't want to do that last time around. I didn't want it to get ugly."

I nodded, though I had no idea what "ugly" might be.

The first time around he'd assumed that anyone—judge, child care worker, or otherwise—who spoke with my mother for fifteen minutes would understand what was going on. And surely, he'd thought, when Mr. Judson visited our apartment—regardless of anything my sisters and I said—it would be enough.

My father had vastly underestimated how predisposed the courts were to keeping children with their mothers in 1977. And how blinding this predisposition could be. He'd also underestimated how very presentable, how calmly convincing my mother could still be to outsiders when she chose.

The day the judge had heard the suit, my father and my mother met with the judge in his chambers. My father came with his lawyer; my mother represented herself. The judge had the report from Mr. Judson in front of him. As he read from it, my father grew increasingly alarmed. Clearly, the judge had already made up his mind to award custody to my mother. So my father, shocked and caught off guard, lost his cool, while my mother sat calmly in her chair, letting him ruin his own case.

"Your mother was so clever," my father told me. "She played the judge by bringing up that trip to Stinson Beach."

I nodded, feeling sheepish. A couple of months earlier, we'd stayed overnight at the beach with friends who had only one spare bedroom. My sisters and I, and Jeni and my father, had all slept in the same room. My mother had, of course, wrenched this information from us when we came home. Now I felt guilty for having told.

The judge, who was in his seventies, had been appalled.

Moreover, my father's cohabitation with Jeni upset him so much that in addition to awarding custody to my mother, he went out of his way to stipulate in his final ruling that Jeni should not be present when we stayed with my father on weekends.

The only good news was that the judge had ordered psychological evaluations of all of us. But even that was not necessarily aimed at my mother. In the judge's chambers that day, when he realized he was going to lose, my father had gone ballistic, yelling at the judge and demanding that he do a psychological evaluation of my mother. "All right, Mr. Flynn," the judge had finally said. "That's exactly what I'm going to do. I'm ordering psychiatric evaluations for all of you, for Mrs. Flynn, for your children, and *for you*."

My father assured me this would change the tide. "Once a psychiatrist talks to your mother, everything's gonna turn."

I nodded, kicking my feet a little against the chair.

"It's going to take some time," he said. "You're going to have to be patient."

I was *it*. I hovered on the concrete patio in front of our building, glancing quickly back at the cans. Bent and weak around the middle from so much kicking, they were stacked in a precarious pyramid. I'd placed them where four lines of the concrete squares of the patio came together like Colorado, New Mexico, Utah, and Arizona. But slightly off-center—so anyone charging down the sidewalk wouldn't have a straight shot. They'd have to slow down and swerve at the last minute, giving me a few extra seconds to beat them to the cans.

I could feel them out there. When I'd counted out the numbers, my voice echoing through the neighborhood, I'd heard most of them run left. But they could crawl down into the street, circle around, and come up on my right. I had to cover both fronts. I walked to the edge of the patio, stopping every three feet to look over my shoulder. I froze to listen for movement, for breathing, for the first footfall. Then suddenly, I made a fast break, ran to the edge of the patio, and leaned over the wall to look down into the street to see if anybody was plastered against the garage. Nothing moved in the street below. The white chalk of the stucco wall was imprinted on my stomach when I stood back up.

As I turned, I caught a flash of red, halfway down the block. Theo slipped behind a hedge as he advanced one bush closer to the cans. Then we were both running. He knew I'd seen him and made a break for the cans. His feet, in long tennis shoes, slapped against the pavement. I was squatting on the ground, clanking the can for the third time when he kicked into my hand. I pulled back. His foot crashed into the bottom two cans. The little kids jumped up and began to scatter. But I still had the top can in my hand. Theo played fair. He sat down on the steps and yelled for the other kids to come back.

I'd already caught the little kids. I'd picked them off fast, sensing them before I saw them, moving from bush to bush, noisy in their stealth. Amy, Allison, Eleanor, Willy, and Frances were huddled on the steps leading up to our apartment building, watching me, waiting for someone to come blasting in and set them free. In most games you only had to catch one person, then they were *it*, and you got to join the fleeing crowd. In kick-the-can you had to catch everyone. You had to catch sight of them, run to the cans, and call out their names while tapping the top can three times. Even then, anyone left in the field could come flying in, kick over the cans, and free all the prisoners.

Willy had made a wild break for the cans almost as soon as I'd finished counting. I hadn't even had any prisoners. He did it for the pure thrill. I'd beaten him easily to the cans. What do you do with dumb boy energy like that?

I'd wanted to catch Sara or Theo or Steven first. When a little kid like Willy was *it*, the game usually broke down. The cans would get kicked over and over, the kid would get weary and hopeless, and end up going home crying, with the boys stalking behind him chanting, *Can't take it, Can't take it* until Sara made them stop.

We'd been outside since we got home from school. We tied sweatshirts around our waists, stretching the cotton sleeves into tight knots, so that when the fog came in we wouldn't have to go inside. My mother stayed in; we went out, slipping through the back hall, past Sara's room, past the newspapers she read every day but could not bring herself to dispose of, folded, stacked, then heaped knee-high, then thigh-high, then waist-high all the way to the door.

We'd grown up some—I was ten, Sara was thirteen—enough to befriend the boys down the block, which would have been impossible a year earlier. We'd kept mostly to ourselves since moving to 24th Avenue, playing Chinese jump rope on the patio, sometimes with friends from school—our friends couldn't go inside the house, but the patio in front of our building, this square of concrete where the sidewalk opened up, twenty feet by twenty feet, gave us a place to be. Or we'd ride our bikes quietly down the block. And the boys would careen past us on their bikes, coming so close they'd almost knock us over, but they never said a word.

The neighborhood girls our age had rejected us. We didn't go to private school; that was probably the main thing. But hand-made clothes, preternatural shyness, and whatever rumors about my mother circulated in the neighborhood couldn't have helped.

Sometime over the previous summer, our games started to overlap with the boys'. No one said hello, no introductions. One day we were all just playing SPUD together in the cul-de-sac at the foot of 24th Avenue. Then we taught them the game we'd brought back from Denver the year before.

Steven, Kevin, and Willy lived down there, in the hulking house at the bottom of the hill, the one whose driveway you were spit out into if you rode your big wheel straight down the alley at the end of our block. They were rich. We all knew that because of the size of their house, which was almost as much of an embarrassment to them as ours was to us.

I'd been in their house a handful of times. A big silent entryway led to a hallway and then a kitchen with an island in the middle and counters all the way around, shiny appli-ances, and Spanish tiles. In one room there was a huge leather couch. That's where they'd sit, scrunched down into the folds, staring at the TV, one hand lost inside a box of Cocoa Puffs. I'd never seen their parents up close—I'd seen them getting in or out of the car in the driveway—in the house there was just the Spanish-speaking maid, shooing them from the refrigerator.

At Steven's house we'd set up the electric race-car track so it ended in midair, high off the ground like an unfinished highway overpass. We'd get the cars whipping around the track and then launch them off the end. Those little matchbox cars flew across the living room.

Steven had a GI Joe. I watched as he walked his doll across the floor, moving one leg and then the other forward in an awkward march. With each step his torso began to lean back, like he was trying to get under a limbo bar. Steven had to keep straightening him out—jerking the body back up on top of the moving legs. GI Joe was so literal. Hard, stocky, lethal. It never occurred to me to move any of my dolls that way. Their pale legs floated under gathered skirts and petticoats as they moved through the air, gliding across the room. Their feet touched the ground only when they got where they were going.

The games at Steven's house were straightforward. How fast can you run? How far can you shoot that car across the room? How long can you let the big wheel roll out of control? No plot, no romance, but then these rooms were not heavy either, at least not with any form of anguish I could recognize.

The six of us made up the core group. The strays we'd taken on—Allison and Aidan, whom Sara babysat for, the Peabody sisters from down the block, Frances from the apartment across the hall who was weirder than any of us because his parents didn't have a TV, and sent him to the French American school—filled out the gang.

We played kick-the-can and capture the flag all summer, climbing through everybody's backyards. Even after school started, we'd meet up when we got home in the afternoons. For Halloween we made a haunted house in the basement of our apartment building, hanging cobwebs and dressing the little kids up like ghouls—we gave Frances a Dracula costume and made him come up out of the dryer, teeth bared, when kids came in. We put on little plays in the garden behind the apartment building, sketches whose humor depended primarily on cross-dressing—Steven in a white wig made from a mop head as Little Red Riding Hood's grandmother. We charged a dollar entrance, and everybody's parents came, even my mother.

We raced big wheels down 24th Avenue. The hill was steep, and big wheels had no brakes or steering—not when you went that fast. You'd just hold your legs in the air, clear of the pedals, and let it roll. The only way to stop was to shift your weight, lean into the turn at the bottom of the hill, and roll to a halt on the flat part of West Clay Park. If you didn't make the turn, you had to roll off the big wheel or crash. Like sledding on concrete. Sara would stand at the bottom of the hill, a bandana for a flag in hand, stopping traffic. She'd calmly explain to the drivers that they would have to wait until the racers were down.

For a year and a half, maybe two, we owned that block. We played outside summer, fall, and winter until well after dark. We didn't ask each other any questions. Boys can be kind that way, at least until they turn mean.

Theo sat on the top step, his long legs tilting up towards his chin, brown hair hanging down to his shoulders. I walked slowly to the far end of the patio. I was more tense now; I had something worth protecting. I watched Theo out of the corner of my eye to see if he'd give away anyone's hiding place with a glance down the street. Theo, who lived directly behind us on 25th Avenue and climbed through our backyard to play with us every day, rounded out our gang. He was a year older than I was; Steven was exactly my age. In the back of my mind, I knew Sara was too old for them and Amy too young, so if it was going to be someone, it had to be me. Today I liked Theo. Other days I liked Steven. It was a constant shuffle. Not that it mattered. I'd never tell anyone, and we never let on that anything like that mattered anyway.

My hand went to the nape of my neck, reaching into the familiar knot. I chose one strand, and slowly pulled it loose. And then another. My mother used to brush out our hair, each one of us, in the morning before we went to school. With time she'd gotten careless, in the habit of just brushing over the top of the tangles in the back. Then she stopped altogether, and each of us was left to struggle with our tangles on our own. A losing battle. On weekends my father would sit us down on the floor in front of him while he wielded the brush from the couch. He didn't know how to brush right. He was not patient. When he finished, there would be a burning circle of scalp where he'd yanked and tugged at my hair. Every once in a while my mother decided to cut our hair. We hated that too. Amy and I always broke down in tears. Tangled as it was, we could not bear to lose any of our hair.

If I could catch Sara and Steven, I'd be home free. I stayed close to the cans, never giving them an opening. For a long time, nothing happened. They were waiting me out, hoping I'd get sloppy and take a risk. I knew if I was going to catch them, it would be through patience, not speed. Sara and Steven could both outrun me. I doubted they could outwait me. I made slow circles on the patio, monotonous and careful, staying within twenty feet of the cans at all times, reversing myself suddenly from time to time in case they were counting my steps. One of them would break before I did.

I stood, bristling, in the living room, as my mother slowly circled my feet, putting straight pins in the hem of a pair of pants she'd just finished sewing for me. She'd called me in from playing outside for this fitting. I couldn't bear to look down, the pants were so terrible. My mother had chosen a light cotton material patterned in an unruly riot of red, white, and blue—in honor of the bicentennial—with lines of stars and stripes running vertically up the legs of the pants. They didn't look like something anyone would actually wear. Maybe, maybe, you'd use this material for a pillow cover. I was not going to wear them. Not to school, not to play outside, not even in the house.

I would have given anything for a pair of blue jeans. I hadn't had a pair for years. Any pair of pants with a zipper would have thrilled me. My mother didn't do zippers. The Butterick patterns she used, with blonde girls with curls or tall, thin, deftly sketched ladies on the cover, looked promising. But I was no longer fooled. Nothing ever came out like that. The elastic my mother sewed in the waistbands made the pants all pooch out around your stomach. The best I could hope for were solid colors, neutral patterns, clothing that would call no attention.

There was no point in telling my mother any of this. I'd say, "Nobody wears pants like this," and she'd say, "If everybody jumped off the Golden Gate Bridge, would you jump too?"

When she finished pinning, she backed away to take in her handiwork. I shifted my feet impatiently, trying not to get stuck with a pin, and averted my eyes.

"You can wear these pants on the Fourth of July," she said.

"If I want to look like fireworks," I said, the words darting out so fast, with such disgust, they shocked me as much as they did my mother.

Her head snapped up. She came quickly to her knees, reached out, and slapped me across the face. Hard. I leaned away from the next blow, but she sat back down, breathing heavily, still tensed. I did not move or cry.

"Don't you ever talk that way again," she said quickly.

"I'm sorry."

"Not ever."

"I won't."

In the shocked swirling moment that followed, while my cheek was in full burn, I absorbed the fact that I didn't have a free pass. She would raise her hand against me just as fast and hard as she raised it against Sara.

In the front hall of our apartment Sara and Amy and I lay with our heads together, in a circle, chins propped on elbows. Spread in the center of the circle was an illicit feast. The Hostess fruit pie I held in my hand had a reassuring heft. I peeled back the wrapper to take a look at the whole thing. It was crescent shaped, slightly squared off, and serrated around the edges. When I took the first bite, the sweetness of the sugar glaze hit my tongue first, followed by a slightly salty taste of crust. Then the pure, pink ooze of the filling.

When you held a fruit pie in your hand, you knew you were going to be filled from the weight of it. That's why fruit pies were always our first course.

On afternoons when my mother went out, after we saw her trench coat disappear around the corner, we'd sneak to the candy store and buy the food she abhorred. The trouble was we never knew exactly when she'd come home. If she was on an errand—to the bank or grocery shopping, which she did herself now, for the most part—we could gage it, predict when she'd be back. Other times she didn't say where she was going. More and more she'd been staying away for hours, coming back well after dark with no bags in hand. But we could never be sure; she could come around that corner at any time.

So we moved quickly. First we scrounged for change— money my mother would never miss—under the couch cushions, or in the back of the drawers of the hall table. We'd shake coins loose through the slots of our piggy banks, fish dimes from the penny bowl in the kitchen. Fruit pies were thirty-five cents each. So when we had a dollar-five we could talk Twinkies, chocolate cupcakes, candy bars, 7-Up.

A Twinkie was the opposite of a fruit pie; weightlessness was what made it desirable. Like all forms of spun sugar—marshmallows, cotton candy—what was desirable in a Twinkie was its emptiness. Perfect and uniform in a way that only a machine could achieve, only a child could love, Twinkies were all artifice and air. I bit in. Foamy cake. White fluff. There was a clarity to these foods, a reassuring neatness. Nothing murky, crunchy, or unknown.

We had chocolate cupcakes too, each one nestled in its molded plastic cup. The frosting on top, chocolate with a neat curlicue of white, was so firm I peeled it away whole, the way a piece of rubber peels off the toe of a tennis shoe.

I got three glasses from the kitchen and lined them up next to each other. I measured out even draughts from the two tall green bottles of 7-Up. We split a Nestlé's Crunch bar three ways. And then one piece each of Bazooka bubble gum—I'd had a few pennies left over at the corner store.

Piled together, my portions, resting on their bright wrappers, gave me a deep sense of security.

We invited no one to these parties. Not Lisa or her sister Naomi, not Steven or Theo. This was private business, something people who got Twinkies in their lunch boxes would never understand.

Dolly Madison was on my mother's list. Hostess was on the list. Hershey's. Coca-Cola. Bazooka. All poison. They insinuated themselves into the home via the weakest link, children lured in, addicted, held in sway for life.

We ate. We took our time. We made Amy run to the window

to check for my mother every few minutes. Afterwards I never felt sick. A little sad, a little let down, maybe, but not sick.

We put the wrappers into the brown paper bag from the corner store. Sara took it outside and threw it carefully away in the neighbor's garbage can, so that there would be no chance my mother would find it.

But she did find the wrappers. Once it was the green and white waxy paper that covered a Hostess fruit pie in Sara's room. Even if the wrapper hadn't been in Sara's room, Sara would have been blamed. She always was. It took so little. And then the whole house was spinning.

Once I was trapped in the bathroom off Sara's bedroom when my mother stormed into Sara's room. She'd found a bankbook from an account my father had opened for Sara to save her babysitting money. There it was, evidence—hidden away somewhere in a drawer—Sara's signature, right next to my father's. He'd signed as her guardian. Proof. She was under his power. Proof. In stark black ink. Sara had crossed the line.

My mother didn't know I was there, and I didn't dare move, didn't dare get in her path. But I could see through the cracked door. My mother's face was mottled. She pushed Sara into a chair, then down on the bed. She wasn't much taller than Sara, but she weighed more. She'd gotten heavy. Sara barely defended herself, and never hit back. My mother sat on top of her. "I will never let you go," she screamed. Sara held her hands in front of her tear-streaked face to shield it from my mother's blows.

The boys in the neighborhood grew curious about the inside of our house. It started with Kevin, who tried to climb up the acacia tree to see in the front windows. Amy thought it was funny at first. She laughed, shaking her tangled mop of hair, and leaned out the window to try to push him down. Sara and I pulled her back inside, closed the window, and pulled the shades down.

After that it became a game, a challenge for them. Willy would try to peek in, following one of us up the stairs when we went in the back door. We got in the habit of opening it just a crack, just enough to push in past the newspapers, in case someone was trailing us. This made them hungry like dogs.

One day as I slipped in the back door I felt someone behind me. I turned and there was Steven, with one hand out to bar the door. His face seemed strange to me. He pushed the door open and started to step inside. Without either of us saying a word, we were suddenly in a physical struggle, me grabbing the door and shoving it into his body to force him back out. He was startled by the violence of my movement and fell back over the threshold. I put my shoulder up against the wood and shoved as hard as I could. But now his shoulder was wedged into the open space, and he was forcing his way in. My feet slid on the linoleum as I struggled not to give way. I screamed for Sara to come help me.

She'd heard the noise and was there in an instant. Both of us braced our bodies against the door, and I pushed his arm back out, thinking if he dared put his hand back in there I would slam the door on his fingers.

I was fumbling with the lock while Sara braced the door,

and nearly had it in place, when the door bucked forward. Steven slammed his whole body into it, laughing now, in a weird maniacal way.

Sara and I stood our ground; we easily outweighed him, but Steven was backing up, getting a running start and throwing himself against the door, over and over, with frightening speed and strength. Every time we nearly had the lock through its narrow barrel, the door bucked forward again. I felt the wood frame strain around my body at each impact. And his laughter, totally out of control now, was just on the other side of the thin door.

Finally, Sara worked the lock into place. Steven threw himself against the door a few more times, as if he couldn't stop, even though he knew he was beat. We stayed where we were, both of us pressed against the wood, worried now that the frail bolt would not hold. Then he stopped. I could hear his labored breathing as he stood there on the landing, then his footsteps as he took the stairs two at a time, his sneakers on the concrete as he ran up the alley at the side of our building and back out to the street.

Sara and I sat down, side by side, hearts still racing, on the piles of newspapers stacked solidly in the hall. My mother was out somewhere, or so deep in her room that the noise didn't rouse her.

"How much did he see?" Sara asked, when she caught her breath.

I sat with my elbows on my knees, face on my hands. "Not much," I lied.

Early in the spring of the year I was in fifth grade, I came home from school one afternoon, opened the door to our apartment and felt a keen disturbance in the air. My mother paced in the kitchen. Amy rushed out of our bedroom to tell me the news. "Sara ran away," she whispered.

Sara had fled before. Twice the year she was thirteen she had taken the bus to my father's in the middle of the week. Both times she'd spent the night with him and then come home the next day.

That night my father called, and my mother sat in the dining room yelling into the phone, while Amy and I pretended to watch *Hogan's Heroes* in the other room.

My mother called me to her. She handed me the phone and walked away. Sara had asked to speak to me.

"Why did you go to Dad's?" I whispered into the phone when my mother had left the room.

"Mom would've killed me."

"Why?"

"There was a can of paint open in the hallway. I kicked it over, and it got on everything."

"I know, she told me."

"I tried to clean it up, but I got it on my shoes, and then I got it on the carpet. I didn't want to wait for the shit to hit the fan."

"She's not mad about the paint anymore. She's mad you went to Dad's."

Sara said nothing.

"So you're not coming back tonight?" I asked.

She started to cry.

"You're staying there?" I asked when she didn't answer.

"Yeah."

"'Til when?" Again there was no answer. I turned slowly, my bare feet against the parquet floor, spinning into the corner of the dining room.

Finally she whispered, "Lor, I can't take it anymore."

I turned again, and the phone cord wrapped once more around my body as the meaning of her words sank in.

"You're not coming back?" She was sobbing now. I cupped the phone in my hand so that my mother would not hear me from the kitchen. "It ain't exactly peaches and cream for me here either," I said, pressing all the bitterness I could into a whisper.

A loud sob rose from her end. I said nothing to comfort her. It was terrible to hear, but I let her cry.

My mother came back in the room. "I have to go," I said. Sara choked out, "Good-bye."

"See you this weekend," I said coldly. I unwound the phone cord from my body slowly before hanging it up. Reeling, I placed the set in its cradle. I looked up at my mother. She was all mine now.

Chapter Thirteen

"THEY'RE FOUR SISTERS. And they live in a tower with an old woman," I said.

"But she's not their mother?" Amy asked.

"No. She found them in the woods when they were small."

"What about their parents?"

"They're dead."

"So we have to run away?"

"Yeah."

We were sitting on our knees on the floor under my bed. It was a school night. It was late. But my mother hadn't told us to go to bed, so we kept playing.

"Can I be Meg?" Amy asked, reaching for the doll. When Sara first left, Amy and I had fought over who got to be Meg. Now I mostly let her.

"She's blind," I said.

"No," Amy started to object, then stopped. She knew I could

quit and go back to reading, and the night would be a desert for her. Her eyebrows furrowed. "Why does she have to be blind?"

I shrugged. "Born like that."

We slept in bunk beds, but we'd taken them apart. My bed, the top bunk, was against the wall. Hers, three feet lower, was pushed up next to mine. To get into bed I had to walk over Amy's mattress and then climb up onto my bed. Under my bed with its long stilt legs, there was a space big enough to crawl into and sit up straight. That's where we played this doll game.

"The tower is very tall. Trees've grown all around it."

"We need a ladder?"

"Yeah, but there isn't a ladder."

"How're we gonna get down?"

"We'll make a rope. From our hair."

The overhead light in the bedroom was on, but we'd pulled a blue wool blanket down over the opening between the two beds. The room that Amy and I shared had a bright green carpet that peeked out in spots from under the layers of toys, clothes, and books. Amy made a nightly ritual of clearing a path for my mother to come in and kiss us good night. The white plastic shelves against the wall were remarkably clean, as the books and toys that might have gone on them were piled on the floor. But in here we couldn't see the rest of the room, and the light was dim, blued by the blanket.

I scissored my fingers and placed them under Jo's black hair. She wasn't the pretty one, but I didn't care anymore. I made a clipping sound, then passed the scissors to Amy.

"All their hair?" she asked.

"Yes."

She clipped Meg's hair. Then she picked up her own doll, the youngest, her namesake, Amy. She pretended to snip the doll's perfect blonde curls. It pained her.

"Shh," I said, suddenly, hearing something from the living room. I froze and listened, my lips pursed together. Amy looked towards the door—her dark blue eyes open wide under a lumpy mop of hair. The dolls in our hands were frozen too, standing up straight, eyes unblinking. There were murmurs from the living room, as if two people were talking. There was only one person there.

I turned back to Amy, my voice lower. "We weave our hair together. At night. When the old lady is sleeping." I imagined what the rope of hair would look like, four different colors woven together.

I caught the sharp scent of smoke in the air. My mother had started a fire in the living room.

We sat the dolls down on the floor. I held Jo's stiff arms, which flexed from the shoulder and made a motion for braiding hair.

"I'm hungry," Amy said, after a while.

"I know."

"We could get cereal."

I shrugged.

"I can go very quiet," Amy said.

I was hungry too—we hadn't had dinner—but I didn't want to risk rousing my mother with a trip to the kitchen. She seemed agitated tonight. Though she was almost never directly violent with Amy or me, it was still best to stay out of her path when she was in this mood. If we didn't call attention to ourselves, she forgot us, and we could stay up as long as we wanted.

Amy lifted the blue blanket from the opening and crawled out over her bed. Her flannel nightgown bunched at her waist, then fell to her ankles as she stood up.

I waited. My right foot, locked under my folded knees, had fallen asleep. I shifted slightly. Pins and needles shot up my leg. I held still to make it stop.

My mother would be sitting on her mattress, which she'd dragged from her bedroom out into the middle of the living room. She'd be feeding papers into the fire. She didn't use the screen. There was a large patch of charred carpet in front of the fireplace, burned black from when she'd fallen asleep and something big had rolled out. For the past few weeks she'd been burning things at night when we were in bed. After years of hoarding, now she was purging. Piles of accumulated mail. Stacks of newspaper from the back hall. Bills. Even things that didn't catch easily, like milk cartons and butter packaging with their waxy coats, eventually went up in flames. If she was staring into the fire, then probably she wouldn't look up or turn to see Amy slip across the hall to the kitchen.

I lifted Jo up to my face. She wore a sky blue dress that went down to her feet under a red and white polka-dotted apron. Clasped to her dress, at her throat, was a red diamond. Her eyes were perfectly round, with drawn-on lashes sprouting from the bottom and the sides, her brows, two thin curved lines. Her nose was dainty, rounded at the end like Amy's real nose. Not like Sara's or mine, which came to a point. The peachy tone of Jo's lips was the same color as my mother's discarded lipsticks, which we still played with sometimes, an almost-orange that women didn't wear anymore.

Jo had shoes and socks and a petticoat when my grandmother had sent her to me three years ago—and a net for her hair. These were gone. Something about the way her bangs were cut straight across her forehead made Jo look smart and practical. I pulled her black hair together, and twisted it into a bun at the nape of her neck. She looked older this way. Like a woman. Like she could handle things. I shook her, sideways, so her weighted eyes tapped open. She looked surprised.

In the kitchen, I knew exactly how Amy would manage the refrigerator. She'd brace the door with one hand, pulling with the other, to mute the noise when it snapped open. She'd take the spoons from the drawer one at a time, careful not to rattle them. She'd open the mouth of the carton and sniff the milk before pouring.

At the foot of the bed amid a pile of toys, books, and clothes, I noticed a stuffed mouse. I crawled over on my hands and knees, with my head down so I wouldn't bang it on the slats of the bed. The blood flowed painfully up my leg. I picked up the mouse. He was about as tall as a grown person's thumb, wearing a perfectly sewn blue suit and red felt hat. The mouse had two black eyes, beady, made from two black beads.

"See!" Amy said, holding up two bowls of cereal when she came back into the room. She was intrepid. She crossed her bed slowly, balancing the cereal in her hands as her feet sank into the mattress. She handed both bowls to me while she slipped back under the bed and pulled the blanket down behind her.

"There's a field mouse," I said, holding up the mouse, "who helps us get out."

"So we don't need to cut our hair?"

"We need the hair. But he's gonna show us a way through the trees."

Facing each other, cross-legged on the floor, we ate. The cereal was good: Wheat Chex held up strong and crisp against the cold milk.

Amy clanked her spoon against the bottom of her bowl.

"Shhh," I hissed at her.

There was a rustling noise in the living room. We froze again. Footsteps. The faint sound of laughter, but moving away, not towards us. She'd gone to get more newspapers from the stacks piled waist-high in the back hall. We were still until we heard a bundle of papers hit the floor. She settled back onto the mattress. Then there was a roar, like wind, or water rising, the sound of flame consuming paper.

"Turn off the light," I said. Amy crawled out and flipped the switch on the wall. I clicked on the plastic flashlight I kept for reading under the covers at night. I wrapped Jo's arms and legs around the bedpost. She went first, slowly winding her way down. The little mouse waited for her at the bottom. Next came Meg, feeling her way, then Beth, then Amy. At the bottom they all linked hands. Then they ran.

Chapter Fourteen

FOR EASTER my father's parents came for a visit, and we rented a house on Stinson Beach for a week. My sisters and I spent all day running from the waves, burning our fair skin, our bathing suits caked with sand. My father taught us to body surf, egging us on, pushing us farther and farther out, his presence, waist-deep in the surf, allowing us to push beyond the threshold of our fear.

My grandfather cut a dignified figure on the beach, tall and thin, his back bent slightly down towards the sand. He took long walks in the mornings when it was still misty and cold. Sara, Amy, and I would go out after breakfast to look for him, but we could never see him against the horizon of sand. We'd play on the beach, beginning to tunnel into the hard wet sand, until finally, with some relief, we saw his form reemerging in the distance. He was old, and we didn't want him to get lost.

At my father's apartment in the city my grandfather seemed

caged. He'd fix things around the house, go to the hardware store and buy wood filler, or a new hinge for a door. But mostly he would just sit very still in the living room during the day, beside my grandmother while she embroidered.

At the beach he seemed more at ease. As he came towards us along the shoreline, we watched him bend and pick up stones from the sand. His arm flared out at his side and traced a horizontal line through the air as he skipped stones into the surf. I couldn't see his hand, but I knew it would be curled, cupping the stone with the surety and grace of a man at ease with things. By the time he returned, reached us on the beach in front of the house, the sun had begun to emerge through the fog and we had built a complex of tunnels that were now flooding with the rising tide.

Amy and I wore matching suits, the same half-cotton tank that had lost its grip around the legs and rode up our butts. Hers was pink; mine was blue. We had matching tummies as well—small round ones that pushed the suits out a little in front. We weren't exactly fat, but we weren't skinny either.

Sara was somehow skinny now. At thirteen, all the extra effort in her body was bent on other ends, sending her upwards in long lines that erased the baby curves. She wore a large T-shirt over her swimsuit to hide the progress that had taken place beneath. She rounded and hunched her shoulders down. Several times a day my father would come up behind her and pull her shoulders back. He wanted us to stand up straight and proud.

Sara had settled in at my father's. The front room became

hers, and she had a chest of drawers and a pile of new clothes. Jeni bought her a wraparound denim sundress. It was the single most appealing item of clothing I had ever seen. I don't remember what we said when we first saw each other after Sara left, only that for a time she and I were brittle and careful with one another. But I could not stay mad at her long. I needed her too much. Plus, it was such a tangle. Nothing was fair. My mother had cast Sara out and clung to me. Nothing either of us did seemed to affect this. Sara had borne the brunt of my mother's rage for two years, perhaps shielding Amy and me. How could I blame her for leaving?

Yet without Sara at home I stood in a perilous grace with my mother. I had to manage her alone. No long hours talking in Sara's room. No one to help measure what we might or might not get away with. No one to exchange looks of warning with. My mother's attention tight upon me. The risk of her discovering that my heart was hardened against her seemed incalculably high. The slightest slip and I would cross the line.

I collected things from the beach over the week: feathers, stones, sea glass, shells. The fine pale grains of sand were velvet between my toes. Stinson was sheltered in a cove, so unlike Ocean or Baker Beach, the ocean was not forever throwing its coarse refuse onto the shore—things were softer here, older, more ground down by time, sun, and care. Peach-colored shells, about the diameter of a dime, were scattered on the sand. A fishing line could be pushed through the opening at the top. By the time the week was over, I'd strung together a tight choker of these shells. It was a pretty thing to look at, but heavy, and tight when you put it on, and when you came right down to it, impractical for actually wearing.

What I loved most was the sea glass. Emerald green, lapis blue. Brighter than stones and shells. Sadly, the smooth stones could not be strung. I collected them anyway, piling them into a bottle during the week, imagining I would come by a small drill so I could make a necklace of them. That was the kind of thing my mother might be talked into. Sometimes she'd throw herself into a project and take Amy and me to the craft store on Geary. She kept us in crayons and glue and construction paper. Once we cut out paper butterflies and shellacked them onto a piece of carved wood.

Sara and I walked down the beach together, and I kept my eyes peeled for sea glass. "Where do you think it comes from?"

"Broken bottles, worn down by the ocean."

I rubbed the jewel-like green glass in my hand and imagined the thickness, the coarseness of a broken green coke bottle. "It's so smooth."

Sara had a rock polisher that was still buried somewhere in her old room at home, a wooden box with a small drawer in front into which you placed the stones. When you turned the crank, the rocks rattled and clanked inside. They were supposed to come out smooth, but we'd never been able to get much more than a slight sheen.

This glass might be a hundred years old. Might have come from across the world, from Hawaii, from China. I imagined women in old-fashioned dresses, so long and heavy they had to lift lace and petticoats when they came close to the water, putting messages into bottles and watching as they drifted and bobbed out to sea. The words, the paper, were gone, leaving only this glass, worn down to its essence—just blue, just green.

In the evenings we sat together after dinner, my father, Jeni, my grandparents, my sisters, and me, reading *Treasure Island*. Each of us read a page out loud, then passed the book along. My father did craggy pirate voices when he read. When it was my turn, I had to pull the book up close to my face to see clearly. The words glided out of my throat. I would concentrate on reading well, pause at all the commas and the periods, enjoying the sounds passing through my throat. I could never hear and read at the same time. So when I passed the book to Sara and listened again I was lost.

We were like foreigners to my grandparents. We lived in a city, ate produce they had never tried, avocados and artichokes. My grandmother was still waiting for the day that my father would have enough money to move to the suburbs, not realizing that for my father, living in the city was to have arrived. That was part of it. My mother was the other part. After my parents married in 1961, when they went back to visit my father's family, ripples of judgment fell around them. My mother not only was not Catholic, she was a minister's daughter. My grandmother's sister refused to come in the house while she was there. And later a cousin actually said to my father, "Well, that's what you get for marrying a minister's daughter." Not my grandmother. She always liked my mother, and anyway my father, her youngest son, was her favorite. In her tough, wordless way she let us know we were, by extension, her favorite grandchildren. She'd raised seven children, six of them born during the Depression. Now she was watching over the lives of thirty grandchildren. Back in Flint, where the auto industry was tanking and the unemployment rate was topping 25 percent, our teenage cousins were in trouble: drinking, doing drugs, totaling cars, and getting pregnant. Our troubles, which were not entirely visible to the eye, must have seemed like the least of it. My grandmother shook her head and clucked her teeth over my mother. She prayed for us. But she had faith in my father. And an eye for these things—she could tell who was going to float. She knew my sisters and I would come out OK in the end.

On Sunday night my father drove us home. I sat up front with him. Amy was in the back, asleep. The radio was on, a classical music station my father liked. I held my backpack in my lap, toying with the zipper. After a whole week away it was harder than ever to go home. All three of us were silent until we reached the bridge. I couldn't tell what my father was thinking.

"It's not going to be too much longer, Sweetie," he said, as he pulled away from the toll plaza on the San Francisco end of the bridge.

I nodded at him, pulling my backpack in against my stomach. "Can I stay with you like Sara?"

He looked over at me, then back at the road. "If you really want to, you can come."

We were both silent. I pushed my feet against the floor of the car.

"Do you want to leave your sister there alone?"

"No," I whispered, pressing harder on the floor.

"We'll be in court sometime this summer," he said.

I took all the sustenance from that promise I could, but I also knew that during the week I was on my own.

My mother was watching for us from the window. She met us at the front door. She hugged Amy and then me. She held me to her for a long moment. Her body had begun to repulse me, and whenever she touched me, I had to resist the urge to pull away. When she let me go, I dropped my backpack on the floor in the hall. She sat down heavily on the piano bench. Amy slipped away to the bathroom. I began my long slog through the minefield of questions she had about the week we'd spent away.

"We had corn on the cob." "We went swimming."

She wanted to know about Sara. About what she wore and how she got to school now. I told as little as I could. She asked about my grandparents. She ascertained that Jeni had been there all week. This felt like particularly dangerous territory.

When she let me go, I went to our bedroom. I took my bottle of sea glass from my backpack and placed it on the shelf at the foot of my bed. If I kept a little water in it, the greens and blues stayed brilliant. Then I slid under the bed where Amy was waiting for me.

I picked Jo up from where she lay. "The tower was really by the ocean. So when they get out of the tree they're on a beach," I said.

"Like Stinson?" Amy asked.

"Yeah, but with cliffs so they can't get off. They walk up and down but they're stuck."

"What do they do?"

"Eat snails and clams. Make bonfires from driftwood."

Amy lay the four dolls on their sides. She pulled their long dresses down over their bare legs. She put Amy's arm around Beth.

"Can we make a raft?" she asked.

I looked around the room, nodding. "We'll have to gather up wood for that."

We moved the three dolls—the three that could see—across the room. They glided across the floor to gather wood. Lincoln Logs were scattered around the room, along with all our other toys. Finding them was like a scavenger hunt. When we found one, the dolls shouldered it back to camp. We clicked the logs together. When it was done, I put Jo on the raft. Her legs stuck out over the ends.

"It's no use," I said.

"The waves are too big," Amy said.

Chapter Fifteen

FOR A LONG TIME I hadn't been able to see the blackboard at school. I couldn't read the list of flavors on the wall behind the ice cream counter, and still my mother ignored the notes sent home by the school nurse.

One afternoon, without warning, my father appeared at the door of my fifth-grade classroom to whisk me to the eye doctor without telling my mother. At the doctor's office there was much exclamation over the degree of my myopia—twenty/two-hundred—not so blind on the scale of things, but bad for a first-time visit. Afterwards with eyes still dilated, wincing from the glare of the mirrors, I tried on every pair of frames at the optician's, and still liked myself better without glasses. My mother had worn glasses since she was a child. She always said it was from reading in bed without the light. And of course I'd done the same thing, read by the shadowy glow of the hallway light, or in the dim circle of the flashlight under the covers.

I settled on a pair of copper-colored plastic frames. When I looked in the mirror, all I could think was: *I look like her*.

A week later, still without a word to my mother (my father thought a fait accompli would be better than an open struggle with her) my father took me out of school again to pick up the glasses. As I stepped out of the optician's with the glasses on, the sidewalk jumped up at me. I reared my head back and to the side, and only slowly learned to look straight at the ground. The pavement was a mosaic of grays, blues, blacks, and whites, some glinting in the sun. Raising my eyes, I saw the sycamore trees that lined the streets were now layered with leaves, each sharp and distinct, where before all I'd seen was the shape of a tree.

I walked home from the bus stop later that day, very slowly, taking in the new texture of the sidewalks, the trees, the cars on the street, but also stalling for time. My father had called my mother to tell her he'd taken me to get glasses. He seemed to think everything would be OK. But I was sure she would be furious with me. Something as important as glasses, something I would wear every day, coming from my father? She'd never let me keep them.

As I started up the stairs in the lobby of our building, the stone statue that stood on the landing loomed over me, a massive Indian goddess, with several arms. "I wouldn't want to be in her path in an earthquake," my father had said years before when we first moved in. I always thought of this remark when I saw her and made it a habit to run up the stairs and get by her quickly. Today I dawdled. I could see the features on her face clearly for the first time. She wasn't as stern as I'd thought.

Before going inside I took the glasses off and put them in their case, then inside my backpack. I let myself in the door.

My mother came to meet me when she heard me come in. "Let's see your glasses," she said. I searched her face for the grim tension that came with anger. I took out the glasses, handed them to her, and then stepped back, half expecting her to smash them. Instead she pulled them out of the case and examined them. She moved towards me. I froze. She placed the frames carefully on my face. "They make you look very smart," she said. And still I waited, sure that the anger would come.

But it never did. Instead we sat down in the living room, me on the couch, her in her armchair, and she told me about when she first got glasses as a girl. Everyone had said, "Boys never make passes at girls who wear glasses," and she'd refused to wear them. She thought that this, along with continuing to read in bed, had made her even more nearsighted.

"Wear your glasses so your eyes don't get worse," she said. "And don't listen to what anyone says."

Then she went to the bookcase and dug out a 1940s hard-cover version of E. S. Nesbitt's *The Enchanted Castle*. The book didn't look all that promising. The dark gray cover with just the title engraved on the front gave nothing away. The corners were dented, the pages rough at the edges. She showed me the inscription inside: for Sally Ann Barton, 1948. She'd won it in a spelling bee in school when she was just about my age.

"This was one of my favorite books when I was little," she said. "You can have it now."

I understood she was giving it to me as a kind of consolation. And of course that made sense. Everyone knew glasses and books went together. Neither of my sisters read the way I did, or the way my mother had, compulsively, continuously, desperate for a new book the minute the last one was finished. And neither of them needed glasses. I would never like the way I looked in glasses, but it was the price I'd paid for entrance into those thousands of pages of enchantment.

I settled into the couch to read, opening the worn cover of the book. The crispness of the glasses was intoxicating, dizzying. The letters were very neat and tight on the page. I looked up and across the living room. Inside our house, so much clarity was exhausting. The formerly undifferentiated mess that covered our floors was now distinct: a pink doll shoe here, the little bulbs from the Light Bright set, Marilyn Monroe's lurid face staring up at me from a magazine in the living room. In fact, the specificity of the books and magazines that made up my mother's Kennedy archive, which was stacked knee deep at the foot of the couch (*Profiles in Courage*, PT109, Jackie, Bobby, Marilyn, Lee Harvey Oswald, Chappaquiddick, the Cubans, the Russians, the mafia—my mother had it all) was suddenly more vividly disturbing. I took the glasses off just to make all those layers of things go away. I pulled the book up close to my face. *The Enchanted Castle* was much better than it looked, and without my glasses on I could limit the world to the small circle of words directly in front of me.

My father gave me a hard-covered composition note-book for my tenth birthday. Until I received it, I hadn't known that I coveted one, so it was all the more amazing that someone had finally given me the right gift. It was a studious-looking thing, bound at the spine, with a black-and-white speckled cover, not like the flimsy colored spiral notebooks we used for school. It seemed to me both old-fashioned and grownup all at once.

I'd already laid claim to a future as a writer. At school and at home, I wrote stories on the wide blue-lined paper we used for practicing our letters. But this notebook put ideas in my head, egged me on. I decided that I would write a novel. The form was there—the book already bound—all I had to do was fill in the pages.

I sat in the kitchen, elbows mashed against the white For-mica of the table, in the middle of the round booth that was built into the corner of the room. The table was cluttered: cereal boxes with their tops yawning to the ceiling, dishes from break-fast, my mother's electric fryer, glistening with grease, perched dangerously near the edge of the table. The cord ran over my shoulder to the outlet behind me on the wall. I'd cleared a foot or two of space to work. The notebook lay open before me, and at my elbow was a sheet of lined paper on which my mother and I had mapped out the chapters of my book. She'd written in Roman numerals for each chapter; I'd filled in the plot. In the first chapter Heidi, my main character, was orphaned. In the second chapter she lived with cruel foster parents. In the third chapter she ran away. In the fourth chapter she lived in a

barn and was befriended by animals. Chickens gave her eggs
for breakfast. In the fifth chapter she was caught by a farmer
and had to run away. In the sixth chapter an old woman took
her in. In the seventh chapter the old woman died, and Heidi
had to run away. In the eighth and final chapter Heidi walked
by her old house and saw a light in the window. Peering in,
she saw her aunt and uncle, who had returned home from an
extended vacation and had been looking for her.

I shifted in the center of the booth, my fingers gripping a
blue ballpoint pen. On the first page of the notebook I'd written "once upon a time." As I looked at the writing on the page
I worried that I'd ruined the notebook, marred it with my poor
script, which despite strenuous effort would not turn elegant.
The letters were bent and cramped, refusing to lean in one
direction; some went left, some right, some bolt upright.

My mother stood at the kitchen counter, smoothing Crisco
on the skins of potatoes for baking. She looked over at me.
"Why don't you write it in pencil first?"

She opened the oven and set three potatoes on the rack. Her
hands glistened from the Crisco. She went to the sink to wash
them and then came and stood over me. "I can read it over
for you, help you with spelling, and then you can do it over
in pen."

She was, despite everything, still a tremendous repository of
knowledge. She helped me with plot refinements, coming up
with a job for Heidi's soon-to-be-deceased father (TV repair
man). Writing, books, and imagination remained safe, the
last unguarded territory I shared with my mother, where on

occasion I was still her charmed child. Her suggestion to write in pencil was the magic word that set me writing.

I worked in this way for weeks, possibly months. I'd clear a spot at the kitchen table to write each day when I came home from school. Some days my mother kept me company. Other days the door to her bedroom was closed and a deep silence echoed from within, broken only by an occasional riffle of laughter, something half stifled that slipped under the threshold of the door, or by waves of laughter, remorseless and derisive, as if she were lording it over the folly of an unseen interlocutor. Then I had to labor on alone while Amy watched TV in the living room.

My mother's sobbing was harder to tune out. Long, sustained cries, which I had to steel myself against or be swallowed by. If I were kind and brave, a good daughter, I would knock on her door, creep towards her bed, crawl in with her, wrap my arms around her, and make her stop crying the way she could still do for me, the way I had once been able to do for her. But I didn't. Instead, when she cried Amy and I slipped out the back door as fast as we could.

Later, when she emerged from her room, when she roused herself to make a meal for us, red-eyed but slowly recovering herself, she'd read over what I'd written for mistakes. I erased misspelled words, added commas, and then went back over the whole thing, tracing the penciled words with a pen.

Looking back over what I'd finished, the pages flush with ink, gave me a very deep sense of satisfaction. There are few things more pleasing to the eye than a page filled with words of your own making. Even now, if I close my eyes, I can see how it looked, page upon page, the narrow lines of blue ink wavering inside the wider, deeply indented gray of pencil lead, the paper stiff from so much handling, furled and rippling from the double layers of script. It took nearly until Christmas to reach chapter seven. I was closing in on my happy ending, though the stages of loss took more time than I'd expected.

One morning I rushed out to the living room, searching for my saddle shoes, desperate not to miss the bus again and set the whole Mom-driving-me-to-school-but-me-never-getting-there scenario into motion. My shoes lay by the side of the wing chair, right where they'd landed the day before, when I'd nudged them off while reading. My socks nestled beside them. I'd pushed those off too, never looking up from my book, my big toe wedged inside the ribbing, sliding them slowly off my feet.

I sat down on the floor and pulled on the socks. I looked up into the grate of the fireplace. A fresh pile of ash one foot deep filled the grate. The scent of smoke was still in the room. The ashes were layered, piles upon piles, the burnt echo of paper, soot still holding form. My eyes locked on a bit of black-and-white speckled cardboard among the ash. My hands froze in midair over the laces of my shoe, one knee still pulled up against my chest. I swallowed hard. I got up on my knees and crawled towards the fireplace. Remnants of blue-lined paper. Yellowed and brown and black. Transformed. Unfamiliar.

My own unmistakable crooked handwriting curling into the charred corners.

I reached in and lifted a piece of the cardboard. It dissolved in my fingers, fell away, raising a cloud of ash. A sound caught in my throat. I couldn't move. My eyes burned. Rage ran through me. Up and down my legs, shivering in my arms, pulsing into my hands. The charred cardboard trembled in my fingers. I heard the toaster pop up in the kitchen and was suddenly aware of my mother. She was opening the dishwasher, rattling the silverware as she took a butter knife from the tray.

The blue carpet swam around me. I was going to scream. Could feel a scream gathering, thickening in my throat. Could feel blood racing. Hot and tight, pulsing at the boundaries of my body, ready to fly loose.

My mother called to me from the kitchen. I pressed my tongue against the roof of my mouth. Swallowed. Swallowed again. I looked down at my shaking sooty hand. I made myself stand, walk to the bathroom. Run warm water over my hands. Spin the white bar of soap between my fingers. Watch the sooty water swirl down the drain. Hold the soap under the water to wash it clean.

I went to my mother in the kitchen. I didn't look into her face. I hated her.

Why did she burn it? Because he gave it to me? Because I clung to it? Maybe she didn't even see it. Just picked it up and tossed it into the fireplace without knowing. I hated her.

She handed me a piece of cinnamon toast. "Be a good girl at school today," she said, and I hated her. She kissed me on the forehead. I stared into the toast. The cinnamon soaked into melted butter made a dark spot at the center of the bread. I hated her. I said nothing about the notebook, not then, not ever.

I took the front stairs two at a time, tossed my toast into the bushes on the patio, hit the pavement running. I hated her. I hated her. I hated her. Blinded by tears, I sought out the cracks between the paving squares. I stretched my legs out in a leap, or foreshortened my stride to land squarely on the lines. I hated her. *Step on a crack, break your mother's back.* I hated her. My feet slapped down hard on every crack on 24th Avenue. *Step on a crack, break your mother's back.* I hated her. All the way up the four long blocks to the bus stop on Lake Street.

Chapter Sixteen

As part of the preparation for the custody case, each of us had to go talk to a psychiatrist. My father picked me up from school and drove me over. I went into the dark office by myself. I sat in a deep leather chair. Dr. Silverman sat behind a huge desk in the dim mahogany of that room. He had a neatly trimmed, dark beard, like every stereotype of a psychiatrist—only I had no stereotype; he was the first psychiatrist I'd ever seen.

"What's your mother like?" he asked once I settled in.

I gazed at him. I wanted to say she's a paranoid schizophrenic. But I hesitated. I wanted to be clear this time. Not make the same mistake I'd made with Mr. Judson. But I also sensed I wasn't supposed to use those words first.

"She's sick," I said.

"In what way?"

I considered again just coming out with it—using the words that had become familiar to me through long conversations with my father. To be on the safe side I dumbed it down a little.

"She doesn't know the difference between what's real and what's not real," I said.

Dr. Silverman's eyebrows went way up. "What makes you say that?"

"She talks to herself. To people who aren't there. And she fights with devils in her head."

"She's told you this?"

"Yeah."

In the end, I told him everything I could think of to damn my mother. In the dark of that office, from the depths of that huge chair, the words flowed out of me. I told him about the house, how very, very messy it was. I told him that my mother got angry, that she threw things, broke things, burned things. I told him we had to live with my father and that he shouldn't listen to Amy if she said she wanted to live with my mother. She was scared and too little to understand. She had to come to my father's too; she couldn't stay there by herself.

He took notes on everything I said, his eyebrows rising and falling as I spoke. I could tell that I had his attention. I only saw him that once. I don't remember what he said to me, if he reassured me or tried to comfort me; all I remember is being sure he knew what I was talking about.

After the notebook was gone, I stopped writing. I put everything I had into the games we played and the stories I told Amy at night when neither of us could sleep. Shadow puppets on the wall in the dark, a teddy bear with a golden heart that was stolen by thieves, an underwater world discovered by the Little Women—the details of the stories came to me in shards, but even now they retain the glittering power of a talisman. I'd lost my older sister, it's true, but together Amy and I created a nearly seamless world of imagination that carried us.

"Maybe we find a bottle in a cave," I said.

"Why?"

"To put a note in."

Amy looked at me hopefully. "Maybe a boat can come find us and take us to Europe?"

It was evening, almost dark; we were home alone. My mother was out. She'd left hours ago and hadn't come back. It was hard to say anymore which was worse—her presence or her absence.

"No," I said. "A turtle will come and take us underwater." I picked up a yellow and green stuffed turtle that I'd won at a coin toss at school.

"Underwater?"

"Yeah."

"Why underwater?"

"It's magic."

Amy picked up a small plastic brush and started to comb Meg's hair, looping it into a ponytail.

"I wanna go to Europe."

"Well, we're not."

"It's not fair," Amy said, her words rising on a tide of anger. "You get to decide everything."

I looked at her hard. This sent her over the top. She grabbed the turtle from me and threw it across the room. It landed near the end of the bed, knocking over a glass of orange juice that had been sitting there for two days.

"Fine then," I said, getting up, ignoring the juice, "be a baby."

She lunged for me as I rose. I caught her hands before the blows landed. I held her wrists tightly up in the air. "Calm down," I said, slowly, looking her in the eye. "Control yourself." She fell away from me in tears, and I left her.

I went out to the living room and looked for my book. I found it pressed open at the spine, on the arm of the green couch. I was reading *The Diary of Anne Frank*. I settled into the corner of the couch, took off my glasses, and rubbed the place where they left their mark. I wasn't used to them yet.

I had to bring the book right up to my face to read without my glasses. But I preferred it this way. The glasses made the letters crisp and tight, the words small, and somehow less potent. I liked to crawl in—take it straight, unmediated by glass.

Amy came into the living room. I didn't look at her. She sat in the big wing chair by the window and watched for my mother. She didn't talk to me, but I felt her remorse, and it tugged at me.

Outside I heard the sound of plastic trundling over pavement. The kids were racing big wheels down the hill in front of our house.

I looked out the window. I couldn't quite see the street. The bottom half of the window next to me was covered with cardboard. There were now five broken windows in the house: this one, two in the dining room, one in my mother's bedroom, and the one over the sink in the kitchen. Each time she broke a window she cut out a piece of cardboard and attached it with masking tape over the broken pane. The acacia tree in the front yard, which hadn't been trimmed since my father left three years ago, blocked the other windows facing the street. It was shady in there all the time.

I heard Steven yell—"On your marks, get set, go." He must have been standing at the bottom of the hill, with a bandana for a flag in his hand, holding traffic at the bottom of West Clay Park until the racers were down. Last summer, Sara had been the flag-holder because she was the oldest. That was last summer, when I liked Steven. Now I hated him.

"What are you reading?" Amy asked.

"Anne Frank."

"Who's she?"

"She's a Jewish girl who got killed by the Nazis."

"Oh."

Since Steven had tried to break in the back door, I didn't play outside anymore. Besides, if they asked me where Sara was, what would I say?

"When's Mom gonna be home?" Amy asked.

I looked over at her, softening now. "I don't know," I said.

"Will you play dolls with me?"

"Later."

"Please."

"I'm reading."

"We'll go underwater. With the turtle."

I sighed. "OK, when I finish this chapter." Though of course she had no way of knowing when I finished a chapter. She was in a special reading group in school. Her class had a green group, a red group, a blue group, and a yellow group, and then "Sam, Tram, and Amy." Sam was trouble. Tram was Vietnamese; he'd just arrived and he couldn't really speak English yet. And Amy was Amy. I was surprised she couldn't read. In nursery school she'd known the names of all seven continents, when she was only four. But then she was a sleepy kindergartner. Now she was in second grade and still hadn't quite woken up. She stayed home with my mother as often as she went to school. That was part of the problem. In any case, her wits were engaged elsewhere. She had an uncanny way of staying out of trouble with my mother. Her strategy was to stay small. She was cagey and innocent all at once. Then again, she was small. She was only seven years old.

Amy brought the dolls out to the living room. She lined them up on the sofa to wait. She brushed Meg's hair again and again with the little plastic brush. Poor doll, her nylon hair was stretched thin.

I finished the chapter—but couldn't put down the book. I peeked ahead. I checked the dates—June 1943. She only had to make it one more year. I knew how it was going to come out, but I still couldn't help hoping, and counting the days.

"One more page," I said before Amy could complain.

"How many words?" She tried to lean over my shoulder to look at the book. I turned the book away from her.

"I don't know."

Amy started to hum a Johnny Cash song. I pulled my eyes loose from the book to smile at her. When she got to the part the radio station bleeped over, I blurted out with her, "I'm the son of a bitch who named you Sue!" The sound of our voices in the empty house made us both feel better. I put the book down on the arm of the sofa, and we gathered up the dolls to take back to our room. We crawled under my bed and picked up where we left off.

"Jo's down by the water trying to catch fish."

"Amy's with her?"

"OK, yeah, Amy's there too. And the turtle comes 'cause he got the note."

I laid Jo across the back of the stuffed turtle. I stretched her arms around the turtle's neck.

"At the very bottom she can breathe."

"So what's this doll game you and Amy are playing?" my father asked me one weekend. It was now a well-established habit that on Sunday afternoons as the hour of our return to my mother's drew near, he and I would sit in the front room for a talk.

I was startled by his question. "It's a game we play sometimes."

"Your sister seems pretty caught up in it." The night before Amy had spent an hour telling Jeni about our game. Amy's complete absorption in the undersea world had raised an alarm.

I shrugged. "It's just a game."

"How often do you guys play?"

"I don't know. Most days." In fact, we played every day from the time we got home from school to the time we went to bed.

"Why don't you take your sister outside to play sometimes?

"Mom doesn't want us to go outside." This was not really true. She didn't track us all that carefully anymore. But it silenced him.

Later that day, as he dropped us off at my mother's, he leaned across the seat to kiss me good-bye and said, "Why don't you guys lay off the doll game for a while. Play some other games. OK?"

"OK," I said, pulling my backpack over my shoulder.

Amy and I ran quickly up the stairs. When we got halfway up, where my father could not see us, I squeezed Amy's arm. "Why did you tell Jeni about our game?"

"I don't know."

"Don't do it again," I said.

"OK."

"It's not their business." I held her eyes a moment, still squeezing. "I mean it."

"OK, OK. I promise," she said, shaking her arm loose from me.

Chapter Seventeen

MY MEMORIES of the last couple of months with my mother are frayed. So much so I feel compelled to fact-check with my sisters.

The showers in both bathrooms in our apartment broke. My mother was not about to let a plumber in the house, so we bathed in a vacant apartment upstairs (one my mother neglected to rent out). Amy and I had to creep up the back stairs of the apartment building in our nightgowns to take showers before bed. My mother moved a portable TV up there, placed it on the floor of the empty living room, and began to watch the nightly news, followed by the Lawrence Welk show (I didn't think that little girl in the chorus looked like me, but we still had to watch it).

Perhaps we spent time in that empty apartment because even my mother was overwhelmed by the devastation of our place. Amy vouches for all this, though somehow in her memory it isn't as bad as in mine. She liked having the clean apartment to run around in, and it never occurred to her to worry what the neighbors thought.

My mother still liked to go to country music concerts but didn't want to leave Amy and me home alone at night. So instead she left us in the car in the parking lot while she was inside. She'd get us a bucket of Kentucky Fried Chicken (McDonald's was bad; the Colonel was all right), and we'd play dolls stretched out in the way back of the station wagon—a street light overhead the only light in the vast parking lot of the Cow Palace or the Concord Pavilion. Amy recalls those nights as well. Though again, she thought it was kind of fun camping out like this.

My mother, who had had no previous interest in sports, took us to a few basketball games that season. The Golden State warriors made it to the playoffs and eventually won the NBA championship. We listened to all the games on the radio. Amy has fond memories of those games as well. I might have enjoyed them too if my mother's intensity about the players and the outcomes of games hadn't had an unnatural feel to it.

She cooked for us at night sometimes—spaghetti, pork chops in the electric grill, or just tomato soup from the can with a piece of cheese melted on the bottom of the bowl. More and more Amy and I foraged for our own meals: toast with peanut butter and jelly, yogurt with fruit on the bottom, and bowl after bowl of cereal.

The kitchen, though, was treacherous. A minefield of rot. Milk went sour in its carton in the fridge, bread molded on the counter, fruit rotted in the bowl, vegetables turned furry and soft in the crisper, and hard-boiled eggs turned sulfurous and evil in the shell.

My mother still made bag lunches for us for school, though the contents were thoroughly untradable—peanut butter and Miracle Whip sandwiches, little boxes of raisins, fruit if we were lucky. When there was nothing decent to put in a lunch bag, she'd give us fifty cents for the cafeteria.

Amy and I didn't have too many "parties," the junk food feasts from the corner store. Money was harder to come by without Sara, who'd always had cash from babysitting. The couches and change bowls were tapped out. And anyway it was way too scary without Sara.

My mother started sleeping in the living room—to keep an eye on the fires that smoldered in the fireplace all night, I suppose. I have a very clear memory of finding her in the mornings with sheets of aluminum wrapped around her body under the covers. She still liked me to come get in bed with her on the mattress in the living room before I got ready for school, an experience that now set my teeth on edge. I never asked about the foil, and she didn't explain. I thought vaguely that it was some kind of beauty treatment. Mostly I tried not to think about it at all. Neither of my sisters will vouch for this one.

When I run it by Sara, she looks at me strangely. "I don't remember that," she says.

"It must have been after you left. When she started sleeping in the living room," I say.

"She slept in the living room?"

"Yeah. She dragged her mattress out there on the floor in front of the fireplace. You don't remember that?"

"I remember the fires." Sara rolls her eyes at me.

I nod, still stuck on the tinfoil. "I'd come out in the morning, and there'd be big sheets of aluminum foil next to the bed. She wrapped them around herself, around her legs and arms when she slept."

Sara is looking at me intently now, but a space has opened between us—as if I'm describing the events of a childhood she had no part of.

"Really?" she asks doubtfully.

"Yeah," I say, sticking to my guns. "Every morning towards the end there. I thought it was some kind of beauty treatment. Maybe to lose weight?"

Sara nods, looking at me steadily.

"Now I think it was more of a protection from outside forces thing. X-rays or voices or something."

"Like the people who put tinfoil inside their hats?" Sara asks.

"Yeah," I say, and then relate a story I heard recently about someone whose mentally ill mother used to cover all the windows in their house with tinfoil.

"Why always tinfoil?" Sara asks.

"I don't know," I shrug. "Maybe it works?"

Things were considerably more cheerful at my Dad's house. He and Jeni had moved in together in a larger flat. They remodeled the basement to make a large bedroom for my sisters and me. When it was done, it was the tidiest place you ever saw—all white walls and module units, built-in shelves and beds with drawers tucked underneath. Jeni bought brightly colored Marieko sheets and spreads for our beds. We all assumed it was just a matter of time before we moved in.

School was also a blessed respite. Though I was still absent a great deal, I always did well, and remarkably, neither my teachers nor my friends seemed to catch on to my troubles at home. Except for the gauntlet of open houses and parent-teacher conferences, my school life was completely cut off from my home life.

Each month I ordered a stack of books through the mail-order club at school. My mother let me get whatever I wanted, and she always wrote the checks. When the books arrived, and I had a dozen or so new paperbacks to lug home, I felt a deep sense of safety. I'd shuffle through the covers, read all the blurbs, and very carefully choose the first one to read. Then I'd pile them at the foot of my bed, my reserves, reassuring me in the morning and again at night before I went to bed.

I did a book report for school on *The Endless Steppe*, a bitter story about a Russian girl sent to Siberia with her family. They endured hard work and cold winters, which killed her father, but in the end she and her mother escaped to America. The book club had lots of books like that—little girls in dire straights. I liked stories with magic better, but these were good in a pinch.

Our assignment was to make a cover for the book. Writing the jacket copy was easy, but I agonized over the artwork.

Drawing was not a possibility—I had no illusions about my artistic abilities. The solution came to me in a flash. I cut out a sun, and colored it bright orange and yellow. I pasted it to a solid white sheet of construction paper. I drew a thin waving line across the paper to show the Siberian horizon, just enough to differentiate the white of the ground from the white of the sky. In the foreground I drew a small stick figure of a girl, almost lost in the snow. Then, and this was the genius of it, I got wax paper from the kitchen and taped a piece over the entire scene. Perfect. The girl was misty now. The sun was still there, but muted and bleak behind the wax paper. I'd captured just the desolation I was shooting for.

Sometime during that year the school bus drivers went on strike. Amy walked to school, so the strike didn't affect her. My school was a fifteen-minute drive away, so I had to take the public bus or get a ride to and from school every day for several weeks. My mother and Lisa's mother arranged to carpool. Lisa's mom took us in the morning before she went to work. My mother picked us up in the afternoon. It did not go well. My mother was invariably late, which was excruciating—I was used to my mother's lateness; Lisa wasn't. In her world, mothers picked up their children on time. Each day as the school-yard emptied and I willed the station wagon to appear, I was filled with shame.

My mother's strangeness was an unbroached topic between Lisa and me. We'd been best friends for three years, and though I spent nearly every school day afternoon at her house, she'd never been inside mine. She was smart enough to know something was up. Then again, my mother somehow still came off as normal enough for Lisa's mother to carpool with her.

One afternoon we waited over an hour, but my mother did not show. We searched our pockets for money. Lisa found a dime, so I called home from a pay phone. There was no answer.

Lisa's mom wasn't due home from work for hours, we didn't have enough change between us for the bus, and it was getting late. Though it seemed unimaginably far, we decided to walk home. We stuck to Geary Boulevard, figuring if my mother drove by, she'd see us. We counted every block. There were fifty-two in all.

We had a lot of time to talk, and somehow the rhythm of the walking loosened my tongue. I don't know what unleashed it, but once I started I couldn't stop. I told Lisa about my mother. About the voices, and the devils, about thinking she was in touch with JFK, and the homemade clothes to protect us. I explained that schizophrenia was an illness, that my mother was paranoid. Lisa feared and disliked my mother, and she was angry about being left at school. I finally told Lisa what was going on partly to defend my mother—to let Lisa see that my mother was sick, not bad.

Lisa listened. She was only ten years old. It must have been quite an earful. But she didn't judge, and she didn't seem shocked. At least she didn't show it. We linked arms at the elbow and walked the rest of the way in tandem.

We parted ways at 24th Avenue. I turned to go home, she

still had to go two blocks up to 26th. My feet hurt from the hard concrete, and I was worried my mother might be mad at me for not waiting for her at school. But I felt light as I walked, lighter than I'd felt in a very long time.

When school ended for the year, Lisa went to Boston to stay with her grandparents for six weeks. Sara was with my father, and we saw her only on weekends. I didn't want to play outside with the neighborhood kids. So mostly I was stuck inside. The summer was interminable. I wrote long letters to Lisa. I read—*The Hobbit, To Kill a Mockingbird*, Nancy Drew mysteries—anything I could get my hands on. And Amy and I played dolls. Despite my father's admonishment, we were even more deeply engrossed.

The Little Women lived underwater now. To keep their feet on the floor of the ocean, to weigh themselves down so they wouldn't float up, they filled the hems of their long skirts with sand. A whole world that nobody knew about flourished down there: castles in the coral reefs, sea glass for money, snails for breakfast, an evil dwarf, an enchanted kelp forest, and sea-horses to catch and tame and ride.

There came a day that summer when once again I was seated on the floor of the living room with my mother, at the foot of the dark green couches, the spot where my sisters and I had once staked our claim on the prairie. The custody suit was to be heard soon, soon, any day now, but not yet. I'd come this far clinging to the prisoner's hatch-on-the-wall faith that what can be measured can be endured. Counting, always counting—

three days to the weekend, two weeks 'til we go to the beach, a month until school starts, ten cars and my father will be here. I'd nearly worn myself out counting, and still the closer we got to the final day in court, the more the time before me seemed to expand.

My mother and I were talking about Hiroshima. Already the names Hiroshima and Nagasaki filled me with sadness. In school we'd made colored cranes from origami paper to send to Hiroshima. But the things my mother told me were new: a bright and blinding light, burns on the bodies, bones without skin, the illnesses and more death that followed. I cannot remember precisely how the conversation went, only that eventually it turned to the possibility of this happening in San Francisco. The Russians, I suppose. My mother said if it came to it, it would be better to die than to survive. If the bomb was to fall here, if we knew it was coming, the best thing to do would be to kill ourselves. We wouldn't have much time.

She trained her clear blue eyes at me and asked, "If something like that happened and I told you to kill yourself, you would, wouldn't you?"

The breath between my lips wavered. I felt the wire that ran between us go tight. Was she talking about a real nuclear attack or some apocalypse only she was expecting? What was the difference? How would I know? A shiver of terror rose in me. I did not want to pledge my life to her.

She waited.

I nodded my head, forced out the words. "If you told me to, I would."

Chapter Eighteen

THE COURT FINALLY HEARD my father's appeal to the custody suit on September 13, 1977—Amy's eighth birthday. I had just started sixth grade. My father was unequivocal about the outcome: he would win. This time he had all the forces mustered: lawyers, psychiatrists, child welfare workers. I believed him because at this point anything else was unthinkable. I had no backup plan, no scheme to run away from my mother if the courts ruled against us again. I was wholly fixed on the decision. It seemed to me I would either go live with my father, or I would perish.

My father was less certain how the day itself would unfold. The judge might want to talk with us before ruling. We had a new judge and this one was kind, he said, and if we had to talk with him it would be in his chambers, not in the courtroom. That did not reassure me. A judge in his chambers—black robes, in rooms hard with wood and sternness—conjured no images of sympathy in my mind. And anyway, I didn't believe I'd get off so easily. I was sure I would have to testify in open court—raise my hand in the air, swear on the Bible, spill our secrets, tell everyone publicly how crazy my mother was. And she'd be there, her eyes boring into me from the other side of the room. She'd find out finally that I was not on her side.

This scene went no further in my mind. It was like a dream, where you come close to the point of death, but you never actually die. What might happen after I crossed that line, I could not imagine.

The principal came to call me out of my classroom around eleven. I felt ill but not surprised. My father had said he might come get me out of school to go see the judge. I followed the principal into the hallway and saw my mother waiting for me in her beige trench coat, hands thrust into the pockets. My stomach dropped. She'd come to steal me away before the judge could rule. Why else would she be here?

I walked numbly towards her. The principal left us standing face-to-face in the long quiet of the hallway. The light was dim, the walls a pale institutional green. Doors to classrooms ran the length of the hall on either side of us. They were all closed. Each had a small window at adult eye level. Behind those windows I could hear the murmur of teachers' voices, students reciting answers in unison.

My mother had written a letter to the judge, she told me. She started to cry. This confused me. Then I was crying too, though I could not understand what she was telling me. She wrapped her arms around me, pulled me to her. "You're going to have to live with your father," she whispered into my shoulder. I sobbed louder. "Just for a little while," she said, stroking my hair. I clung to her and in the same moment willed her to go. Just go away. The more I willed her to go, the harder I cried.

"We'll be together again, soon," she said, "very soon." We stood there for several minutes until she began to pull away, still crying. She patted me on the shoulder. I couldn't bear to see her cry.

"Go back to class now," she said.

"OK," I whispered, hoarse with tears.

"I love you," she said.

"I love you too."

She turned to go. I watched her move heavily down the hall. Her coat billowed behind her. Then she turned into the stairwell and was gone.

I walked down the long hallway, past my classroom, past the sound of Mrs. Raymond's voice, and the clack and scrape of chalk on the blackboard. I went into the girls' room. In the stall I fumbled at the metal latch until it fell into place. I sat down on the closed lid of the toilet, pulled my legs up, rocked myself, and cried.

A very long time passed. When I stopped crying, when I could see again, I read all the graffiti on the walls of the stall. *Deanna + Marky 4 ever, Rachelle fucked Danny W.* We were in sixth grade; it was turning nasty.

In front of the mirror, I stared at my eyes. Puffy. Red. Impossibly bloated. When I walked back into my classroom, everyone would turn to look, follow me with their eyes until I reached my desk. I wondered how long it would take until I looked normal. Like I hadn't been crying. I pulled brown paper towels from the dispenser over the sink, ran them under warm water, and pressed them to my eyes. The warmth took away the sting, but the paper was coarse against my skin.

My father was waiting for me in the schoolyard at the end of the day. Somber in his suit, fresh from court, he put an arm around my shoulder. We walked slowly across the yard together. He explained that my mother had not shown up in court. She'd sent a handwritten note to the judge saying that she was no longer contesting the custody suit.

"I guess she knew she couldn't win," he said, shaking his head, his voice strained. He seemed sad, but not surprised.

I was stunned. I'd never considered the possibility that she would stop fighting. If there was one thing I thought I could count on, it was her will to hold us to her. All these months I'd been bracing myself against her. Her will, her anger, her ferocity. Now she'd given way. I tumbled headlong into unfamiliar territory—territory I would inhabit for the rest of my life—where my pity for her was rapidly outpacing my fear.

"Of course you can still visit her whenever you want," my father said. I looked up at him sharply. Blinking back tears, I looked down at the ground. We stood inside the grid of a four-square court, near the front gate of the schoolyard. I tried to imagine a time when I would want to see my mother.

"Listen, it's still your sister's birthday. Your mother wants you and Amy to spend the night with her."

She'd made a cake, bought presents and ice cream. My father said we could stay with her overnight, get our things together, and he'd come for us in the morning before school.

I rubbed my shoe along the outside line of the four-square court.

"You don't have to go if you don't want to."

"She'll be mad."

"I'll tell her I won't let you go. You don't have to say anything."

I nodded up at him, flooded with relief that he was going to take the hit for me.

My mother's two brothers had flown out from Denver that afternoon. My father had asked them to come. He didn't know how my mother would react to losing custody of us and didn't think she should be alone. He'd just come from picking them up at the airport, then rushed to talk to me before my mother came to get me from school. He hadn't had time to drop my uncles at their hotel, so they were waiting in his car.

As we came out of the schoolyard, I saw the brown station wagon parked at the curb. Amy looked at me from the back-seat—already her face had that frozen look she got whenever Mom was mad. My mother came out of the driver's seat fast, furious that my father had gotten there before her, anger hardening around her mouth at the sight of him.

I don't remember what they said to each other. Her anger. His firmness. Me staring down at the speckled gray and white sidewalk, trying to look like a hostage. Eventually, she got back in her car, convinced he was not going to relent.

"Wait for her to leave," my father said. "I don't want her to see Tom and Peter with me." He shook his head. "She'll go nuts."

We stood on the curb, but my mother did not pull away. She sat in the driver's seat watching us. Our mistake was imagining we could put one over on a person whose suspicions were perpetually aroused.

My father let out a train of air. "Let's walk. See if we can lose her."

We walked in the opposite direction from where he'd left his car. She followed, the brown station wagon creeping alongside us as we walked. My father glanced back over his shoulder. He had a plan. "This is a one-way street. We'll take her down this way, then double back." He winked at me. Strategy, cunning, these were his strong suits. I felt better. We were both walking as fast as we could. Then we were laughing. I felt sick to my stomach. And giddy. It was so ridiculous, her trailing us, us trying to get away. Anyway, I was safe as long as my father was there.

At the corner we turned, doubled back, and then raced around another corner to where he'd left his Mercedes.

As we got to the car, the station wagon came around the corner from the opposite direction. My mother stopped the car in the middle of the street, head-to-head with the Mercedes. She came out screaming, calling out her brothers' names. "Thomas," she wailed, "Peter," she screamed as they piled out of the car.

I stood on the sidewalk looking from my father to my uncles

to my mother. I watched my father raise his hands as if to calm the air under his palms. "Take it easy, Sally," he was saying, "calm down." But she had blown; his words were gas on fire. Her anger flared and rose, flickering back and forth between my father and my uncles. Their presence here confirmed for her that they were all in contact, were in fact conspiring against her, that her brothers had perhaps played a part in this plot to take us away from her, perhaps were even planning something worse: to put her away.

Tom placed a hand on her shoulder. She rolled away in fury, and turned her eyes on him. All three men were over six feet tall. At five foot seven, there was no way she could have loomed over them. Still they cowered. She lunged. They dodged.

"Sally, Sally," my father repeated as if it were a plea, a complaint. Then very quickly he turned away from her towards the station wagon, whose driver's door was wide open to the street. He opened the back door. "C'mon, Ame," he said, and pulled her out by the arm in a way that made me worry it would come out of joint. My father hustled her over to the Mercedes, calling to me as he moved, "Laura, get in the car."

I pulled my door closed; it slammed with the heavy Mercedes thud. Amy turned saucer eyes up at me.

"Tom, Peter, let's go. Sally—enough, you'll see the girls another night," my father said as he slammed his own door shut.

Tom and Peter were still on the sidewalk, trying to talk my mother down. My father started the engine. He leaned across the passenger seat, rolled down the window. "Tom, Peter, let's just go," he yelled again. Finally they obeyed. Peter got in front, and Tom in back with Amy and me. My mother hovered at the window on the passenger side, her face a mask of rage, the lines in her forehead carved; furrowed channels ran down either side of her nose. Her eyes were wild behind her thick glasses. She pounded a fist on the side of the car as we pulled away from the curb.

Amy pressed in against me in the back seat. My uncles were shocked, embarrassed, and frightened. They'd never seen my mother this way. Her family, living at a safe distance in Colorado, had tended to downplay her illness. I don't know if they'd ever trusted my father's version of events up until then. Some part of my mind, the part not frozen with fear, was saying a silent *you see* to them.

"We should never have let her see us with you," Tom was saying.

My father didn't answer.

"She's following us," said Peter.

I turned in my seat, and looked back through the black defrost lines of the rear window. My mother maneuvered a ragged three-point turn in the narrow street, then she pulled out behind us.

What happened next I have logged in my memory as "the accident," but of course it was exactly the opposite of an accident.

Our car slammed forward. My body crashed into the driver's seat, my neck whiplashed forward. Amy fell into the space between the front seats. My father's arm came out to stop her.

"Oh, my god," said Tom.

"Holy Christ," my father said, looking into the rearview mirror. "Hold on."

Our car bucked forward again. The second time my mother rammed her car into ours was not as violent; she was already hard on our bumper. Amy hung onto me so we went as one into the back of the driver's seat. We put out our arms against the seat back, bracing ourselves for another blow.

My father made a fast right turn onto Geary Boulevard, into flowing traffic to try to get away from her. She came right after him, careening into us from the side as we made the turn. Amy and I were thrown over against the door, then over onto my uncle as we lurched back. We scrambled to right ourselves as my father stopped abruptly at the corner.

We were at a full stop when my mother slammed into us. Then she put the station wagon into reverse, backed up, and slammed into our car again.

People on the corner, waiting for the bus, put their arms in the air, raised hands to their mouths. I could hear their reactions, muffled through the window, first shock, then shifting to the higher pitch of horror as they realized what they were witnessing was not an accident.

Two more times my mother put the car into reverse and slammed into the Mercedes. Each impact sent a wild spike of adrenaline up through my stomach to my heart.

My father got out of the car, and for one sickening moment, he was in her path. She jerked forward, pulling around our car. He jumped onto the median in the middle of the street.

She kept coming, after him, away from us, running the car, squealing, up onto the median. The front tires of the Oldsmobile lumbered up over the curb. My father dodged back, off the median, into the lane of oncoming traffic, slapping a hand on the window of her car to push away. The station wagon came back down off the curb onto our side of the street. She screeched past us, and I watched the station wagon shimmy away down the hill.

Inside our car was very quiet. Outside people were yammering and pointing. Outraged. Shocked. Telling each other what they had just seen.

My father came to the passenger door, which my uncle opened. "Is everybody all right?" he asked.

I looked down at my body. My knees hurt, and my wrists were jammed. Nothing broken, nothing bleeding.

"We're OK," I said for Amy and myself.

We followed my Uncle Tom out of the car, Amy first, then me, feet sliding across the seat. We were stopped outside the Sears and Roebuck department store. I glanced just once at the mangled rear of the Mercedes; the bumper hung loosely on the ground. We were blocking a lane of traffic on a busy street— cars were backing up behind us. The drivers would take a long look at us, then fight their way out into the second lane.

People on the street offered themselves up to my father as witnesses. "I saw the whole thing," one man said. Another proffered a slip of paper on which he'd written my mother's license plate number. My father took the paper. Vaguely, I hoped he would not tell anyone that we knew that number by heart. I was keeping a good distance from all this. The roaring in my ears, the pressure in my veins, the pain in my wrists provided a barrier between these people and me.

I understood that the police were coming. I understood that nobody was going anywhere soon. But I stayed alert. I watched the cars coming towards us on Geary, keeping my eye out for the lumbering brown shape of my mother's station wagon, which I could spot two blocks away.

My father put an arm around me. "You OK?" he asked. "Yeah," I said, holding out my hands. "Just my wrists hurt." He made me bend my wrists back and forth several times. Then, satisfied that nothing was broken, he handed me a dollar. "Why don't you take your sister inside and get something to eat from the snack bar."

"OK."

"Take your time."

"OK."

I took Amy by the hand. She was wide-eyed but not crying. Together we walked through the double glass doors into Sears. The anonymity of the department store swallowed us instantly. A Muzak version of "I'm on the Top of the World" was playing over the stereo system. Involuntarily, I filled in the words: *And the only explanation I can find.*

In the children's clothing section mothers were picking out back-to-school outfits for their children. I held Amy's hand tightly. "Everything is going to be OK," I said. Saying this, having to take care of Amy, was good. It gave me something to fix my mind on. I pulled Amy onto the escalator. The snack

bar was on the second floor. We rose slowly into an overpow-
ering smell of popcorn. Amy looked at me—her face revealed
nothing.

We stood in a long line at the concession stand—teenagers
buying slurpies, mothers with strollers getting snacks for their
kids. Large white and yellow appliances circled around us. A
front-loading washing machine with a glass window was running. We stared into the white swish of water and clothes.

"How come Dad didn't let me go with Mom?" Amy asked.

I turned from the washing machine to look at her.

"He's got custody of us now," I said, stammering across this
gulf.

"But how come he had to make her mad?" she asked. "Mom
bought ice cream. She made me a cake."

I looked into the tumult of the washing machine. Then back
at Amy. We were almost to the front of the line. There was
nothing to say. That's how it is sometimes. You think you're in
something together; you think you know exactly what's going
on in another person's head. Then you get a long, dizzy view
in, and you realize you have no idea what's swirling around
in there.

When we got to the front of the line, Amy wanted candy-
coated peanuts. I let her pick. It was her birthday. The lady
behind the counter handed over a small red and white striped
paper bag. She had no idea that my mother had just slammed
her car into ours. Seven times. I led Amy back to the escalator,
still holding her hand. We ate our peanuts. Nobody looked at
us. My heart was still thumping. My wrists ached. My whole

body was still a jangle of nerves and adrenaline, but nobody in Sears could tell. The worst thing you can imagine could happen to you. Five years, five days, five minutes later no one's the wiser unless you tell them. There's almost no limit to what you can shelter within you.

PART THREE   *Sea Level*

Chapter Nineteen

SAN FRANCISCO is surrounded by water on three sides, but ocean on only one, so the name Ocean Beach is not as redundant as it sounds. The coastline here straightens so you can see beach for miles in either direction. Sand slopes away from the concrete retaining wall for fifty yards and then gives way to the Pacific, big and blue and thundering. Twenty-foot waves break far out and then break again and again until they are tame enough to lap and bubble onto the shore. The tide here changes so drastically that sometimes the water comes clear up to the wall and that fifty yards of beach is gone.

When I was a child I thought all beaches were that big, all salt water that cold. Ocean Beach dwarfed all beaches to come.

First memory: my father and mother on brightly colored beach towels high up in the sand. Fully clothed, they keep their bodies close to the ground to stay out of the wind. My father's head is propped on his bent elbow; my mother's head rests on one pale arm extended straight out in the sand. She wears a man's loose shirt over her stomach, which is still soft from giving birth. Their bodies, turned towards one another, form a curved *V* in the sand. Amy, a newborn, wrapped in a soft cotton blanket, is sheltered in the space between them.

Sara and I flirt with the tide. She is six; I am three. Barefoot, we dance on the wet corridor of sand that sparkles in the sun each time the water pulls away. The beach is strewn with great long ropes of seaweed, curling, hairy, monstrous things with impossible waterlogged bulbs larger than my father's fist.

"Go ahead, touch it," Sara says.

I bend down and touch the widest ropy part, just resting the tips of my fingers on the kelp's brown surface. It doesn't move. It's slippery but firm under my fingertips.

We grow brave, hefting its hollow limbs on our shoulders. We watch the line it draws in the sand as we drag it forward.

"Let's wash it off," I say. I want to see it shine.

The sun is out, which makes the day bright but does not make it warm. I'm wearing green polyester shorts and a cotton T-shirt with tiny green and white stripes, a brand-new outfit my mother has just bought for me—perhaps to make up for the loss that's come with Amy's birth. For the first time in my life, her eyes are not constantly upon me.

Sara and I drag the kelp to the water's edge. When the tide retreats, we place it in the hard sand and back away to watch. The water laps at it, tentatively at first, licking the sand from the skin of the kelp, then more insistent, pushing, nudging, recognizing its own. The kelp quivers under its force.

A large wave sends us squealing up the beach. Our feet have long since frozen, but this one threatens our calves and thighs. On the dry sand, we turn. The kelp is gone. We wait for the tide to flow back. Then we see it, caught in the curling, pulling spot where the receding water meets the next wave. The kelp lies on the tight sand, resisting the water funneling under its weight.

Kelp like this, giant kelp, grow best in cold, shallow waters like those off the coast of Northern California. The brethren of the giant sequoias that once lined the coast, the kelp too grow in groves, forming vast underwater forests. Each plant latches onto a rock, holding fast, then sends huge, stem-like stipes to the surface where the broad, leathery leaves receive the sun. Kelp make use of every wavelength of light and can grow up to twelve inches in a day. But they hide their greenery with a brown so brown it masks the bright chlorophyll. It's the smaller weeds, the winged kelp, sea palm, turkish towel, devil's apron, sealace, and tangle that flaunt their colors.

My father's voice comes, sharp and crisp, across the wind and noise of the surf. We turn to look at him. He stands on the towel, his brown hair, which he wears below his ears, blowing straight up in the air.

"Sara," he yells sharply, "hold your sister's hand."

Behind him I see my mother, sitting upright on the towel, straining towards us, the tension of her body an exclamation point on his words.

My parents don't see Sara's face as it flashes first surprise, then dismay. At six, she takes the business of taking care of me very seriously. She grabs my hand, our fingers interlace. My

mother nods at us firmly, her eyebrows locked down in concern. Sara squeezes too hard.

We dance back into the surf after our quarry. In one brave
charge, Sara leading, we each grab hold of the kelp with our
free hands and scamper backwards, bent forward at the waist
over our haul. We make it two feet, when another wave rolls
up and we drop our prey again to run to safety.

The water splashes against our churning legs. Sara runs
slowly so I can keep pace. My shorts are dark green where they
are splattered, and strands of my hair clump together where
they are wet. My hand is stiff in Sara's frozen grip.

This time the kelp has hardly moved. The last wave looked
big, but it didn't pull hard. Emboldened, we spring forward
together. Reaching down in the swirling water, I grasp the
skinny end of the kelp at my feet. I have it firmly in my hand
and pull hard, thinking Sara will grab the thicker end. I see the
wave approaching, but it doesn't look that big. Sara tugs at my
hand, I pull back, willing her to lift her end of the kelp.

"We just looked away for a minute. We were watching the
baby," my father will say with a rueful shake of his head whenever this story is told later.

The wave slams into my chest and throws me on my back.
Sara's fingers slip through mine and I go down into freez-
ing water. I'm inside a powerful darkness, eyes clamped shut
against the saltwater. I'm dragged along the bottom, against
sand and coarse pebbles, then lifted, only to be pummeled
again by a force that rolls me and holds me under.

My father drags me from the surf coughing and choking. I

hit the air panicked, arms and legs wild, the saltwater tearing at my nose and throat, more terrified than I've ever been. My mother pulls me to her, wraps me in her huge orange beach towel, and rocks me in her lap until I can breathe again.

When I get home that day, I stuff my new outfit, my shorts and green and white T-shirt, far into the back of a dresser drawer. I'll never wear them again.

"It was the meditating, that's what started it," my father says, or "It was those goddamn Edgar Cayce books." Or, softened by a glass of wine, he'll say, "Maybe if I hadn't gone into real estate, if I hadn't worked full-time, if I'd been home more . . ."

My grandmother blamed my mother's crazy diets. "I just don't think she got enough vitamins back then," she'd say, her blue eyes brimming over, "it made her susceptible . . ."

I thought it was the apartment we moved to when I was six. Later, in college, in the first flush of feminism, I said, "Maybe at a different time, if she'd worked, if she'd had choices, if she'd found something to believe in . . ."

In the end, these things we tell ourselves, the names we give the loss we cannot fathom, the demon we fear may still come back for us, are as sad and as small as a child's sea-soaked clothing trying to absorb an ocean.

In my family we've lived our lives as if we are still on that beach. If Amy is always the baby, if Sara never lets go of the small hand entrusted in hers, if my father is always strong enough to drag any of us from the surf, and if I am willing to drown, won't she be there too, my mother, whole and waiting, on the shore?

People talk about how fast life can go from good to bad. How one day you're happy, everything is going fine, and then something happens. Someone dies or someone leaves. There's an illness or an accident. Life as you know it slips away. But it can go the other way too. You can go from god-awful to pretty OK in a single day. That's what happened to us, and it was just as jarring.

After that day in front of Sears, I didn't go back to my mother's. I didn't pack a suitcase or bring my books or the Little Women. My father took us home, and I began living with him and my new stepmother. My father and Jeni had gotten married a few weeks earlier, and overnight we were a nuclear family again—almost. Jeni was everything my mother was not. She worked full-time and had a successful career. She was organized, neat, and punctual. She took care of things. Dinner was at seven, a cleaning lady came on Tuesdays, and there were vacuum lines on all the carpets when I came home from school. We were normal—stunningly, blindingly so.

We had to get all new clothes of course, which was exactly what I'd dreamed of. Only it didn't go as I imagined. Jeni was always the one who took us shopping. (Poor Jeni, she was thirty-five years old and inherited three daughters—eight, eleven, and fourteen—just in time to see us all through adolescence.) All I wanted were jeans and T-shirts. Jeni favored a more buttoned-down look and wasn't used to buying clothes for kids. She'd pull blouses with little peter pan collars off the rack and ask what I thought. "That's nice," I'd say, my face revealing absolutely nothing. I'd lost the ability to be direct, to risk asking for what I wanted. Instead I let her take the lead and then ended up hating the new clothes almost as violently as the old ones.

I had one very good year, though. In sixth grade we were the oldest in our elementary school. I was in "gifted," and my little clique of friends was in charge of the school talent show. We were on an "independent learning system," which from a practical point of view meant we were frequently excused from class to go across the street to Sears to buy slurpies for our teachers or down to the school auditorium for unsupervised rehearsals. We spent a great many hours refining the moves on our ensemble "Hustle" for the talent show.

The euphoria did not last. By seventh grade I was in a new school, separated from my friends, and almost overnight I seemed to lose my ability to speak, at least outside our house. The sadness of my separation from my mother caught up with me, or maybe it was the long hand of adolescence, which got hold of my voice box. Whatever it was held on for six years.

At first my mother called every night. Then less and less. The phone calls were wrenching, like being forced back underwater when you'd gotten used to breathing air. At the end of each phone call she would say, "I love you." And I would echo her, with a mechanical, "I love you too." When she stopped calling altogether, relief was the only feeling that rose to the surface.

The year after my father got custody of my sisters and me,

my mother's brother sued to become her legal conservator. The courts declared her incompetent, and my uncle was given legal power over her finances. She owned the apartment building where we'd lived, part of the settlement from my parents' divorce. My uncle sold the building so that she'd have money to live on, and she was forced to move. This enraged her further, and she cut us off, swearing none of us would ever know where she lived again.

As a teenager, I was only vaguely aware of these events. Twice in the aftermath of the court proceedings my mother was picked up by the police on what is known as a 5150, a request from a family member that a relative be held for psychiatric evaluation. Twice the doctors who interviewed her confirmed a diagnosis of paranoid schizophrenia. And twice, after determining that she wasn't a threat to herself or anyone else, they released her after seventy-two hours. That was the law in California: no one could be institutionalized against his or her will. No one could be forced into treatment unless there was imminent danger. My father recalls going to see her once while she was being held at Langley Porter, the psychiatric hospital. She was strangely cognizant of her own situation. "I'll be out of here by tomorrow," she told him. "I can fool all these people."

"Why not just stay, let them help you?" he asked. She laughed at him.

We were at the legal limit of what could be done. I recently learned that while I was in high school in the 1980s, my uncle seriously considered kidnapping my mother and taking her to Colorado, where he and the rest of her family lived. The laws there were different. She could have been forced into treatment. My uncle was in contact with someone who would do the job, the kind of person you would hire to kidnap and deprogram your child from a cult. In the end, he lost his nerve. It would have been a felony. And he must have doubted whether he really had the right. My mother had always been able to get by on her own. In retrospect, the psychiatric determination made all those years ago has proven accurate; strictly speaking, since she lost custody of us, my mother has not been a danger to herself or anyone else. She's lived a life of almost unspeakably limited circumstance, but it is *her* life.

Most of all, I think my uncle was afraid. My mother would never have forgiven him. She was ferocious. I can still see her standing on the street in front of my school that last day, her body nearly shaking with rage under her trench coat, daring him to defy her. She cowed all of us into doing nothing. In the end the ferocity of her anger, the steeliness of her will, protected the disease. As if the true battle she waged was on behalf of the disease, as if her mission was to let it run its course unimpeded. It's the only battle she won.

At home with my father and stepmother in the years that followed, we spoke less and less about my mother. What could we say? We were powerless, and you can only rub your nose in that kind of pain so much. My father was determined to move on. I was the hardest case: a moody, serious teenager, a bookworm in a family of tennis players. I brooded over my mother. I could not banish two thoughts from my mind. She was suffering—the echo of her sobs behind the bedroom door stayed with me—and she was alone. My initial relief at being free morphed into searing guilt at having abandoned her.

Sometimes, when I couldn't sleep at night, a blood-chilling thought crept into my head: *What if she is right? What if my father is the devil?*

By the time I got to high school, I was terribly shy, socially isolated, and convinced that the one person who might have given me guidance was gone from my life. If she had been the one with the magic touch for me, then shouldn't I have been the one to be able to reach her? I was not the oldest but had been the last one close to her. I felt horribly responsible. I was far too terrified to take any steps towards seeing her, but I skewered myself for what I believed was my own cowardice.

What I did do was scour bookstores for information on psychology and mental illness. I was drawn, over and over, to the *Diagnostic and Statistical Manual of Mental Disorders* in the school library. The first time I hefted the book from the shelf, checking to make sure no one was looking, I sat at the back of the library, as if I were doing something dirty. I thumbed through the pages, my heart pounding, until I found what I was looking for. The entry was cold comfort. Most of it I already knew: the symptoms, the categories, the prognosis, embarrassing, awful, and grim, respectively. Then there was a section on genetics.

I'd gotten wind of this already, but the statistics stunned me: the children of schizophrenics had a 30 percent chance of inheriting the disease. Thirty percent. Almost one in three. I was one of three—bookish, solitary, I even looked the most like my mother. I knew, just knew, that if anyone were taking bets back then, they'd have bet on me.

My sisters and I would visit my mother's parents in Denver every couple of years. What I remember best about those visits is morning chats with my grandmother at her kitchen table in the long, slow hours between breakfast and lunch, while my grandfather was out. The smell of bacon, the fat still solidifying in the frying pan on the stove, lingered in the air. Their house was always over-climatized, too cold in summer, too warm in winter. Sadie kept the television on low. The sound of Phil Donahue pestering his audience made a companionable hum in the room.

When conversation turned to my mother, as it inevitably did, Sadie would bring out the pictures. She would tell us how darling and stubborn my mother had been as a child, how bright and elegant a young woman. "You girls just can't imagine how much potential your mother had . . ." Her voice would catch in her throat; a few tears would gather in the corners of her very blue eyes and roll over the loose skin of her cheeks. Sitting across from her, I would fiddle with the pink packets of artificial sweetener she kept on the table for coffee and iced tea. I lined and realigned them in their dish. We would sit, transfixed in silence for a few moments. There were no words for the loss that lay always between us. It bound us and, sometimes, made it hard to be together. As my sisters and I grew older and came to resemble my mother, it was impossible for Sadie to look at us without thinking of my mother. I can say this for Sadie: she never avoided the pain. She let her sorrow show.

My grandfather was considerably more stoic, but the loss was just as devastating. I have a letter he wrote to my mother in 1979—two years after my father gained custody of my sisters and me. He wrote to my mother via her bank, which was for many years the only point of contact any of us had for her.

"Sally," he wrote, "I have spent many hours thinking about our past relationships and can think of things I have done that would be changed if it were possible. But, whatever I might have done to alienate you, forgive me. Mother and I want so much to be in touch with you."

He and my grandmother were flying to San Francisco for three days in hopes that she would contact them. He closed the letter by giving her the phone number of the Holiday Inn where they would be staying. "We will be waiting for your call."

My grandparents were both close to seventy by then. I'm guessing they sat in their hotel room all weekend, and the call never came.

My mother's family did eventually manage to reestablish contact with her. My uncle and my grandparents visited San Francisco periodically, and she would meet them for dinner. But that was all she'd allow. Until she died, my grandmother always sent my mother gifts for birthdays and Christmas and regular letters full of family news. I have no idea if my mother opened them.

I didn't see my mother from the time I was eleven until I was twenty-three. I finished high school somehow, then college with considerably more success, without a word from her. I was always a good student, and as soon as I went to college, again almost overnight, I shed the shyness that had shackled me for six years. I held a part of myself in reserve, but I learned to live in the world. I felt, not unlike I had as a small child, that there was a great disconnect between my inner and outer life. There was the daily business of classes and friends, of romances and campus politics, and then, set completely apart, was my inner world, a large share of which was dedicated to my mother. I locked myself into a grief that seemed to be the only thing that still tied me to her.

Once on a road trip to Chesapeake Bay with college friends, we found an old wooden swing set along the road. The swing faced west. The sun was low in the sky. As I pumped my legs into the air, my feet stretched up and out over the water, I had the feeling I was swinging straight into the sun. It came to me in that moment with a rare and physical certainty that my capacity for joy was as deep as my capacity for sorrow.

After I graduated from college, my sisters and I did reestablish tenuous contact with my mother via the bank. We were grown, and she was no longer the wrathful specter of my memory and imagination. Smaller, meeker, harmless, she was not better, just calm.

She still wouldn't tell us where she lived. We knew, though, because years earlier my father had enlisted the help of a friend, who trailed her from her bank to a residential hotel in the Tenderloin, in the grimy heart of San Francisco. From time to time over the years, my father had discreetly checked in with the manager of the hotel to make sure she was still there.

Since we didn't want to alert her to the fact that we knew where she was, we still used the bank to contact her. Once or twice a year, to arrange to meet her for dinner, one of us had to drive out to the Wells Fargo near the end of Geary Boulevard, where she'd had her savings account for the past thirty years. We'd wait for her to show up—a specter in a beige trench coat. That we could count on. Like clockwork, every second Friday between five and six o'clock, she'd go to withdraw just enough cash to cover her expenses.

When it was my turn to stake out the bank, I'd try to time it just right. Getting there late, missing her, or not knowing if I'd missed her and having to gird myself for a second trip, was awful. Waiting was awful too, so I'd get there at the last possible moment.

She lived alone, shrinking further and further into herself with each passing year, like an imploded star. She remained, willfully, outside the mental health establishment. She has never, as far as I know, taken medication. She's kept to herself, stayed out of trouble, and refused any help. She had enough money to live on—but she parsed it out, taking only the bare minimum. By the time she was in her sixties and I was in my thirties, her illness made no material claim on my life. It was only when I'd get in the car to go meet her, when I began to imagine how much further she would have deteriorated this time, when I felt a familiar leadenness in my limbs, that the full psychic weight of the situation was upon me.

Her bank was out in the Richmond District, where I grew up—San Francisco's most westerly, fog-prone neighborhood. Even though she didn't live out there anymore, she was a creature of deep habit, and she never changed banks. The bank had changed on her, though. Her account had once been across the street, but the Crocker Bank, with its sturdy old San Francisco name, was now long gone, gobbled up by Wells Fargo in the 1980s. After the buy-out, my mother's account had been transferred across the street to a sleek, modern outpost of the Wells Fargo behemoth.

I found an open meter in front of Joe's Place a block from the bank and scrounged for quarters, feeling rushed, nervous, and vaguely remiss. Joe's Place was just across the street from Gaspare's, formerly Vince's, our old Italian standby. Joe's Place hadn't changed: same steamed windows, same tilted ice cream cone on the neon sign, same waffle cones behind the counter. We'd gone for ice cream after dinner at Vince's nearly every week from the time I was five until I was eleven, first with both parents, then just with my father when he came to get us on weekends. Now, the scent of those waffle cones rose to meet me on the sidewalk, carrying a wave of nostalgia so dense it stopped me in my tracks. I could see myself trying to peer up over the counter, having to squint to see the flavors listed on the wall. Orange sherbet, or peppermint stick? I shook off the memory. Right then, I didn't want to feel that small.

Generations of tellers had come and gone from this Wells Fargo. Then came the ATM outside, which made most of their jobs obsolete. More recently, to lure the clients back in or save on rent, they'd put a Starbucks in the lobby. The tellers stood behind a long counter at the back of the building. Up front to the right was a dry cleaner's and to the left the Starbucks—counter, fireplace, seating area, and all.

I got in the coffee line and was grateful once again for the minor miracle this Starbucks represented. I was mercifully inconspicuous in my task. A girl in front of me ordered a caramel latte; she was a friend of the girl behind the counter. They were both teenagers, Asian, chatty. My foot tapped in what probably looked like impatience. I kept looking over my shoulder to make sure my mother didn't slip past me. When finally my mocha was pushed across the drink shelf to me, I clutched it gratefully and sought out a table near the window.

I pulled out a book, a prop really, because I wouldn't be able to read. Instead I watched out the full-length window for the 38 Geary coming from downtown. Each time a bus pulled away, I searched for her trench coat among the passengers left standing on the curb in the small cloud of diesel. It was winter, dark before six, and had been raining all day. I checked my watch— 5:25. I pulled out my journal, wrote the date, wrote *Wells Fargo*, underlined it, tapped my foot. On the street the cars rushed by, four lanes of traffic, tires flickering over the wet pavement. I stared down at the journal. I let it fall closed, and reached for the cell phone in my bag. I pressed the speed dial and called Sara to talk me through.

I've long understood that schizophrenia is a disease that entails changes to the brain, that it's chemical, that it's physical, like cancer or diabetes. You hear of a person battling cancer. You even hear of a person battling alcoholism. But even today, with the rising awareness of the physiological basis of mental illness, it's still more common to say a person *is* schizophrenic, rather than that she's battling schizophrenia. With cancer, in the mind's eye we see the person, whole and healthy, fighting an invasion of malignant cells. With alcoholism, there's the person and there's the bottle. They're separate and at odds, or bound in a dance to the death, but still distinct. Schizophrenia wraps itself so tightly around the personality of the sufferer that the person and the illness look like one. We cannot see the partner in this dance.

I'm now at least ten years older than my mother was when she first began to show signs of her illness. Even by my most conservative calculation, I've aged beyond the period of risk. Also, the statistics on the likelihood of inheriting schizophrenia have been revised. The last time I looked, the odds of falling ill if you have one parent who suffers from the disease were 12 percent. The books are much more tactful these days; in the next breath, they always point out this means you have an 88 percent chance of *not* inheriting the disease.

Still. A few years ago at a writers' conference in Oregon, I was staying in a college dorm room. I put my glasses on the bedside table. I reached to turn off the lamp. I opened my eyes and the ceiling had become a three-dimensional web of light. I blinked hard. It wouldn't go away. Panic seized me. *God, no.* I hurled my body towards the lamp, grabbing for my glasses in the dark. The florescent light flooded the room. Through my thick lenses I peered up. Even in the light, I could still see the broad white lines crisscrossing the ceiling, rounding the wooden beams, giving dimension to the web. Glow-in-the-dark paint. Dormitory interior décor.

Sara picked up on the third ring. "I'm at the bank," I said.

"She isn't there yet?"

"No."

I could hear Sara making dinner for her kids: the sizzle of something frying, the spatula scraping the pan, the TV news, and my niece asking questions in the background.

"Got your coffee?"

"Yes," I said.

Then we talked about the Starbucks, which we couldn't get over. "You remember before?" Sara asked. "How we had to hang around in the lobby and the security guard would come over and ask what we wanted?" I groaned. I remembered. It felt significant, naggingly so, and paltry, at the same time. My mother was crazy; she was not going to get better. There was almost nothing we could do to help her. She wouldn't even tell us where she lived. To see her we had to drive out to this lonely branch of Wells Fargo. But then there was this Starbucks—as if whatever force was organizing the universe had tossed us a crumb: *Can't help you with the big stuff, but I'll put a Starbucks in the bank so you'll be comfortable while you wait.*

Sara and I were still talking when I caught sight of the trench coat: beige, full-length, billowing in the wind, instantly recognizable. My mother, now sixty-six but looking at least ten years older, was crossing the intersection. She glanced quickly back over her shoulder. Her gait was stiff, a little uneven, as if one leg had become shorter than the other. It was always like this. Just when I was about to give up, when I'd decided that she must surely have come the week before, she appeared. My heart jumped. "Oh shit," I said to Sara, "gotta go."

"Call me after," Sara said, hanging up.

I went outside, and we met on the sidewalk. "Mom," I said. She looked up. She took a little step back, then said hello. She used my name, which startled me. She used my name so rarely, I sometimes wondered if she could even tell my sisters and me apart.

"We wondered if you wanted to meet for dinner?" I said. The words came out quite naturally. A calm, efficient part of me took over. Managed. But as I stood there, face-to-face with her, I couldn't help but take in how sallow her skin was. Her once-dark hair was nearly all gray, her scalp visible along a wide swath of her part. She was thin now, having lost all the extra weight she'd carried when we were kids. Her skin sagged over sunken cheeks. My sisters would ask how she looked. "Worse," I'd have to report, "much worse."

"When do you want to meet?" she asked. Her words had a clipped, rushed quality.

"Next Monday?" I offered.

"OK," she said. "We'll meet at the St. Francis?"

"Yes," I answered, though this went without saying. For twelve years we'd been meeting in the lobby of the St. Francis Hotel on Union Square.

"How're you doing?" I asked, trying to hold her another minute.

"Fine, just fine," she said, moving away from me.

"Do you want to get a cup of coffee or something?" I said, motioning back towards the Starbucks.

"No, I'm fine. See you next week," she said, fluttering a pale, curled hand at me, and she was gone.

There's an emotional numbing, a kind of dulling down, they say, after years of schizophrenia. Typically delusions, hallucinations, and agitated behavior decrease with age, almost as if the disease burns itself out over time. What remains is ghostly. The psychiatric terms are chilling and, in this case, accurate: *catatonic mannerisms, flattening of affect, robot-like fixity, petrification of attitude and reactions, poverty of ideas, passivity, a narrow range of modes of behavior.*

A popular misconception is that the flatness results from years spent in institutions or on medication. But my mother's never had the drugs. She's part of the control group, and it's a bigger group than you might think. Statistics on the numbers of untreated mentally ill are hard to come by, but one survey in Baltimore found that fully 50 percent of people who suffer from schizophrenia receive no medication or ongoing psychiatric care.

In the lobby of the St. Francis, Sara and I sat in high-backed armchairs and waited for my mother. Amy called in on the cell phone. She was parking. She was running late. She'd just finished law school, from which she graduated summa cum laude—a long way from the remedial reading group. She was now a public defender and very busy. But she'd be there. My niece and nephew, five and eight years old, were playing in the revolving door of the hotel. Sometimes my mother didn't come. When she did come, she was late. Always we worried. The fact of the matter was she could die and no one would contact us. There was no point in saying this out loud. I turned to Sara and said instead, "Maybe she had other plans?" Sara looked at me, deadpan, shrugged. "Maybe she's busy?" Then we were both laughing, in a hollow-bellied, helpless way that almost loosened the lead in our limbs.

My niece, attracted by our mirth, ran over to us. "What're you guys laughing about?"

"Nothing, baby," Sara said, putting an arm around Kait, whose bear cub arms wrapped around my sister's waist.

If my mother came, we'd go across the street and eat an over-priced Italian meal. She'd stay with us for an hour and a half, maybe two, until she got restless and we knew it was time to go. She'd speak every now and then—answer a question, as long as we didn't pry. Nothing personal, nothing about the past, nothing that explicitly acknowledged that we were her children. My mother carried on the pleasantries of conversation as if out of old habit. She talked most easily with Amy. (Because Amy was still the baby?) Occasionally, she laughed. When she was silent, my sisters and I filled in, telling each other about our lives for her benefit. (Sara and I brainstormed safe topics for conversation via cell phone on the way over.) My niece and nephew knew she was not quite right. They chatted her up anyway, telling her about dolphins and dinosaurs, about art projects at school. They're troopers, not least of all because Sara is exactly the kind of mother my mother was when we were small.

Someone once said that having a relative with schizophrenia is like a funeral that never ends. Certainly, the woman I knew as a child is gone. Yet there is no grave, no stone, no eulogy, to mark her passing. When a parent dies, a child may be comforted by the thought that the parent's spirit is watching over her. We kneel at gravesides to address our prayers, our grief, our anger, our words to the dead. I can't address my mother, not in this life, nor in any other.

Of course, there are people with schizophrenia who recover and others who have good periods and bad. For some, medication makes all the difference. For my mother, I don't even think words like *recovery, cure,* or *improvement.*

I worried over small things instead. Maybe, just maybe, we'd get her to a dentist someday to relieve the discomfort that was obvious from the careful way she chewed. Sara and

Amy thought I was crazy. They focused on new glasses. "That could be done without anyone actually touching her," Amy said. When we broached it, when we broached anything, my mother said, "No, that's OK. I'm fine."

After dinner, she walked us all back to the parking garage under Union Square, across from Macy's, where we'd left our cars. Amy casually asked my mother if she needed a ride anywhere. I smiled. I knew what the answer would be, but I admired Amy for never giving up. At the entrance to the garage, we said our good-byes. My mother never said "I love you," or "Take care of yourselves," or any of the other endearments she'd used when we were kids. Just an awkward pat on the shoulder and "Good-bye." Cars pushed their way in and out of busy downtown traffic on either side of us. I kissed my mother's wilted cheek and turned to go. She stood there until we were gone—made us walk away from her—to ensure we didn't try to follow her home, I suppose. Kait ran ahead to push the button for the elevator, and then we all waited, anxious now to get to our cars, our homes, our lives. But I knew if I looked back, I'd see my mother still standing there on the sidewalk, a shrunken figure in a long beige coat, caught in the glare of the department store windows across the street.

I never wanted to see any light in the sky or hear any rumbling from the universe. I used to tell myself that if the voices ever came, I'd shut myself up, refuse to listen. I wanted to stick to what can be seen and proved, to be sensible and skeptical like my dad. As if we can choose. It's physical. It's chemical. It's beyond our control. This, if you can get your head around it, is not comforting, but it is liberating.

There's the tragedy of my mother's life, irredeemable. There's the echo of this tragedy on my life. That's my business to redeem. And there, bouncing on my sister's lap, is my bright-eyed five-year-old niece. Such a bold and happy child. Might I have been that way? No, I don't kid myself about this. My mother's illness is not the only thing that shaped me. I would have been a brooder no matter what. Some things we come with. Others we are given. The world throws up its beauty, throws up its charm. I have no heart for skepticism, and no amount of brooding will change this.

I worry over big things too. I find I still believe the things my mother told me when I was small. I believe we each have a soul, precious and indestructible, and I worry over where, precisely, my mother's soul resides.

Chapter Twenty

SEVERAL YEARS AGO I visited my father in Paris. He and his wife were living there for a few months. Knowing I was always hungry for information about my mother, he offered to take me to the hotel where they'd met more than forty years before.

As we walked through Paris, his face was grim. For my father everything that touched on my mother was weighted with dread. But as we made our way through the winding streets of the Latin Quarter, I began to understand that this was a pilgrimage. When I first arrived in Paris, my father had said, "I'll show you the Stella on Friday." I hadn't thought about the date. May 10, 2002. By chance, by his design, or simply by the elegant, nagging symmetry on which the unconscious seems to insist, we made this trip on my mother's sixty-fifth birthday. Normally her birthday was a private day of mourning for me. Perhaps because I was jet-lagged, and in Paris, I forgot to grieve until I saw the date on the morning paper.

It was a gray day. From time to time we had to pull up the hoods of our raincoats against the light rain. Normally he and I had plenty to talk about, but today we walked mostly in silence. Neither of us mentioned the date. Occasionally, I asked a question to try to draw my father out.

We walked up Rue Monsieur le Prince, a narrow street lined with bookstores and small cafés, leading to the Sorbonne. "How did things look back then?" I asked. He lifted his head and glanced around. "Pretty much like this." I shut my eyes, and tried for a moment to conjure up the scene, movie set–style, with cars from the 1950s, women in skirts, and men in hats. "Well, how did people dress?" I tried again.

He stopped, and with a gesture of the hand to indicate the entire street before us, he said, "You saw a lot of black." He laughed mildly. There was still a lot of black; leather jackets, black pants, the black bowling/tennis shoes with white stripes that the students were wearing. In 1960 all that black must have been striking. My father arrived from the technicolor of Southern California and landed in the most sophisticated place on earth, in the midst of the original black turtleneck moment.

Suddenly, the Stella was on our right. I backed away to take in the façade. It was pretty, though the stone front was cracked, and unlike the buildings on either side, it had not been cleaned or refaced in recent years. On the second story, white wooden shutters hung loosely in their frames. Black iron patios decked the third-story windows. A few bright red geraniums potted on those tiny decks added the only color to the building. The Stella was still a cheap place to stay on the Left Bank.

We entered through a narrow hall. Three-hundred-year-old wooden beams came up through the brick of the walls and ceiling at odd angles. There was no one in sight, so we started up the stairway into almost total darkness. The stairs were steep and uneven. The settling of the building, the wear of hundreds of years of footsteps, had carved deep wells into the surface of the wood.

My father was briefly enlivened by the task of figuring out where his room and my mother's room had been located. Renovations had been made, tiny rooms joined to make larger rooms and bathrooms added. He went up and down the stairs trying to get his bearings. He showed me the door off the stairway, now locked, that once led to the WC he and Joe had shared with all the residents of floors one and two.

Finally, we decided his room must have been on the first floor just off the stairway where the reception area was now. Still no one had appeared, so we tested the door. My father pulled it slowly towards him. It glided open. Just as promised, the open door blocked the stairway down. My father, speaking in the church whisper we'd both adopted when we entered the hotel, said, "She kind of peeked her head around the corner." He inclined his head slightly. "I invited her inside," he smiled. "She came right in," he said with a lightness I had not seen all day.

In the spring of 2004, out of the blue, my mother called my father one morning to say she was being evicted and needed help. I was halfway across the country in graduate school. By the time Sara and my father arrived, the sheriff was there. My mother was locked out of her apartment. She didn't even have her glasses on.

After some wrangling with the manager and offers to pay all the back rent, Sara and my father realized these people were not going to relent. The manager was glad to be rid of her. After twenty-five years in that apartment, they put her out. If she hadn't had anyone to call, or the presence of mind to find my father's phone number, she would have joined the throngs of people with mental illness who live on the streets of San Francisco.

Within three hours Sara had settled her into a building my father owns nearby, fulfilling my father's prophesy of nearly thirty years earlier: "You'll end up living in one of my buildings in the Tenderloin."

This change felt briefly better. She knew that we knew where she was. Sara bought some new things for her—towels, sheets, and blankets. The manager at the new building kept an eye on her. We'd know if anything happened. This change also made her life real to us for the first time in twenty-five years. Her refusal to allow us to know where or how she lived had relieved us of responsibility for her in some sense.

The next Christmas I was home for break and went with Sara to ask her to meet us for dinner. We knocked on the door. She took a very long time answering. She was not dressed, wearing only a T-shirt and underwear. She was rail thin. She seemed confused but agreed to meet us. On Sunday, she didn't show at the St. Francis. She'd not shown up on other occasions, but this time I was very worried. Was she sick? Could she even leave the apartment? If not, how was she eating?

I called Sara and convinced her to come with me to bring my mother groceries the next day. As we were on our way to the store, Sara called the apartment manager to make sure we could get in; coincidentally, he said, he was just about to call. My mother had knocked on his door the afternoon before and asked if there was anyone in the building she could pay to go to the store for her. She'd given him a couple of dollars for milk and bread.

Sara and I went into the grocery store, overwhelmed by our task. Could she cook? Would the food rot? What does a person need who never leaves her apartment? In the end, we bought all the same foods we'd bought when we'd done the grocery shopping when we were little—Campbell's tomato soup, Orowheat bread, Laura Schudder's peanut butter—choosing brands as carefully as we'd done then, the labels she favored instantly recognizable after all these years.

When we got to the apartment she looked terrible. She had a bruise on her cheek, and she couldn't focus her eyes on us. She didn't have her glasses on, and the light in the apartment was off. We began to wonder if she could see at all. Again she was not dressed, and looked downright emaciated.

"I'm just a little under the weather," she said. When we began to press, to ask what else she needed, she got panicky, pushing the door shut. "I'm OK. I'll be OK, I've just been a little sick, but I'm feeling better."

Then followed a series of consultations between my sisters

and me, and calls to various social service agencies. Meals-on-Wheels had a three-hundred-person waiting list. A city services person I reached on the phone lectured me that the first thing that needed to happen was some mental health treatment, and then when she trusted people again, other steps could be taken. I found my voice rising. "I don't think you understand the situation." Sara had a woman ask, "How can we help her if she won't open the door?" They were the professionals. Weren't they supposed to tell us what to do?

Finally, after many phone calls, we did get her on the Meals-on-Wheels circuit. A blessing beyond compare. We found an optometrist who made us a pair of glasses by guessing at her prescription. She never wore them. We could see the bedding Sara had bought the year before neatly stacked by the door, still in the package.

Sara got a sympathetic social worker to visit my mother. "When was the last time you saw a doctor?" the social worker asked my mother through the cracked door. "Mind your own business," my mother said, pushing the door closed. I could just hear the intonation of her voice. Angry, slightly singsong. Final.

We debated, briefly, the notion of hospitalizing her. Were we allowing her to suffer? She might have cancer, might be dying, might be in great pain. We decided against it for now. Clearly she didn't want to move, and she probably would not be able to tolerate prolonged human contact. Isolation was the route she'd chosen and one we had accepted, to some extent, all these years. We had to ask ourselves, if she'd indeed been suffering from a disease of an organic nature all along and we'd never forcibly intervened before, how could we justify hospitalizing her now when she was too weak to defend herself?

We've settled into a routine. One of us, usually Sara or Amy since I am only in town a couple of times a year, brings her a bag of groceries (toilet paper, soap, milk, bread, peanut butter, cereal) every week. Meals-on-Wheels brings her two meals a day. If for some reason she doesn't answer the door, they call and we know to go check on her. She's improved slightly, is at least not half starved as when we first intervened. Her vision seems better. But she still hasn't left the apartment. "Would you like to take a short walk one of these times?" I ask. "I'll think about it," she says. I report her response to Sara, and we briefly take heart. Then it becomes a weary joke. Sara sends me up to ask: "Would you like someone to come once in a while to help clean the apartment?" She's thinking about that too.

"You know there's nothing keeping us outside that door," Sara says. "We could walk right in. She can't stop us."

"I know." But something does stop us.

On a recent trip home my fiancé came with me when I went to see my mother. He's a poet. We met while I was in graduate school in Minnesota, where I now live. Mike was in California for Christmas to meet my family for the first time. He offered to come up with me to my mother's apartment. "No, wait in the car," I said. She was the one member of the family I was not ready for him to meet.

She took a long time answering my knock. Then she stood half hidden behind the door, looking not at me but sideways at the wall. No matter what I asked—can I take out the garbage, do you want to go for a walk, can I change the sheets—she said, "No, I'm all right." Or "I'm OK now." She spoke as though she were grasping at language, at the habits of speech. All she wanted was to get that door closed, for me to be gone.

Finally, running low on questions and stamina, I prepared to go. I bent over to push the grocery bags I'd brought inside. She stood there in her underwear, mostly hidden by the door. When I raised my eyes I had a very close view of her naked, shockingly thin, old woman's leg, inches from my face—pale, nearly hairless, curving in rather than out at the thigh. The sight of it was like a blow to the plexus. She closed the door and I backed away, stunned.

The image stayed with me for days. *That is your mother's leg*, I told myself each time it rose in my mind. Only I didn't believe it. Seeing her nearly naked made me realize that over the years she'd become an abstraction to me—a cloud of pain, guilt, and despair, detached from physical reality. Her body had not existed for me since I was eleven. And no matter how hard I tried, I could not put this leg together with the body I knew a very long time ago—a body that bore mine, a body that echoes in my own. We are the same height, she and I. Or we were—she is hunched and shrunken now and seems several inches shorter. But I grew into that same build, pale white skin, with dark hair, fleshy in the thighs and hips. I tried to put myself in her place, to imagine what she thought about, what she felt, the same way I'd imagined what she thought or felt when she was twenty-three or thirty-five. I didn't get very far. I had nothing to go on, and my brain locked down somewhere soon after trying to imagine the physical pain she might suffer. A failure of empathy? A failure of imagination? A self-preserving refusal to open myself to any more suffering? I don't know. I just know my brain will not conjure up anything. That door is closed. Something very powerful stops me from breaching it.

Sometimes I wake in the night with a searing vision of my mother's life. In that stark moment of waking I am unable to shield myself from the utter barrenness of the last twenty-five years. Everything that bears on her—the past, the present, and all the time in between—feels like a wild tangle of weeds, wrapped round my throat, dragging me down, holding me under. Over the years, I've had to fight my way to the surface over and over again. To take a knife, cut the hem, let the sand fall out, and rise to the light.

I've always floated. I don't know why. This much I do know: I am buoyant. The sun comes out; I get better. The world outside me, with its joys and sorrows, sorrows far greater than this personal loss, presses upon me. I can only stay stuck in my own sadness so long. These may be the real consolations—optimism and resilience—happy traits slipped into my hand.

Sara called me shortly after that visit. I was in the car driving home.

"Hey, I wanted to tell you this before I forget," she said. "I had kind of a long conversation with Mom the other day."

"A long conversation?" I said doubtfully.

"Well, a few sentences back and forth."

"What'd you talk about?" I felt a slight twinge of jealousy that Sara had managed that.

"I told her some stuff about the kids, and I told her about Mike coming out to visit for Christmas."

"You did?"

"Yeah, she actually seemed interested. She asked me questions."

"What did she ask?"

Sara paused for a moment, trying to remember. "She asked if he was special."

I was stunned. "She did?"

"Yeah."

"What did you say?"

"I said he was. Oh and then I told her he was a poet. It was kind of funny. She had the exact same reaction that everyone else has—that kind of confused *Oh*."

I laughed, because I knew exactly the reaction she meant.

Other times I go back. I see us at the Tea Garden in Golden Gate Park. The tiny cups, the shiny rice crackers, the bitter taste of jasmine tea, my feet dangling under the table. I am five. I look out from inside the teahouse at the arched wooden bridge and I suddenly have an odd feeling, akin to déjà vu, that we are inside the Willow plate pattern, the blue and white china plate pattern with the image of a wooden bridge, a teahouse, a willow tree, and a pair of doves flying overhead. My kindergarten teacher brought the plate to school and told us the story. A young girl was supposed to marry a rich man, but she fell in love with her father's clerk instead. He sent her a message via a dove; she floated him a letter in a paper sailboat. The night before she was to marry, the lovers ran away together. Her father pursued them, and they were both killed. But the gods had pity, and the lovers were reincarnated as doves, the pair flying together over the wooden bridge in the Willow pattern.

I tell my mother the story. She smiles at me. This is the kind of story she likes. I look down under the lacquer table, and see her foot in slightly worn heels gently lifting my own and setting it to bounce.

Russ, Laura, Amy, and Sara in 1976

Acknowledgments

DURING THE SIX YEARS I worked on this book, many people encouraged and supported me. I am grateful to them all. Nina Goldman, Cindy Shearer and John Curtis talked, listened and sustained me when I first began to write. The University of Minnesota Creative Writing Program, The Loft Mentorship Program and the Fishtrap Imnaha Writers' Retreat provided strong writing communities. Thanks to John Witte, editor of the *Northwest Review*, for originally publishing portions of chapter nineteen (in a different form).

Patricia Hampl coaxed me to care about every word. Charlie Baxter told me it was done when I needed to hear it. Julie Schumacher, Madelon Sprengnether, and Patricia Weaver Francisco gave critical feedback, advice, and encouragement. Readers and writing companions Rachel Moritz, Amanda Coplin, Brian Malloy, Jennine Crucet, Ann McWoodie and Sari Fordham spurred me on. Special thanks to Joni Tevis for riding to the rescue, along with David Bernardy, at the eleventh hour.

I am indebted to Maria Massie for confidently shepherding this book into the publishing world, to Amy Scheibe for beautiful editing under difficult circumstances, to Beth Partin for painstaking care of the manuscript, and to Nicole Caputo for the gorgeous cover. Thanks to everyone at Counterpoint for believing in good books, and for their enthusiasm and hard work on behalf of this one, especially Jack Shoemaker, Charlie Winton, Roxanna Aliaga, Sharon Donovan, and Abbye Simkowitz.

I could not have written this book without the love and support of my family. To Jeni Flynn I am grateful for many years of excellent step-mothering—and especially for putting a roof over my head during the first nine months of writing. Thanks to Joe Keith for telling me stories about Paris, Lisa Adelson for standing by me all those years, and Lee Flynn for unflagging enthusiasm for this project.

My father, Russell Flynn read drafts even when it pained him, made sure I got all the dates and numbers right, and always, always believed I was a writer. My sisters, Sara and Amy, have given me a lifetime of solidarity. I am grateful beyond words to all three of them for sharing their memories, letting me tell this story, and for tolerating with grace this appalling invasion into their privacy.

And finally, to my husband Mike Rollin who raised my spirits for the final push, and suggested the title—everything is better when you are here.